G. W. F. Hegel

Twayne's World Authors Series

German Literature

David O'Connell, Editor
Georgia State University

TWAS 862

G. W. F. HEGEL (1831)
Courtesy of the German Information Center, New York.

G. W. F. Hegel

The Philosophical System

Howard P. Kainz

Marquette University

Twayne Publishers
An Imprint of Simon & Schuster Macmillan
New York

Prentice Hall International
London • Mexico City • New Delhi • Singapore • Sydney • Toronto

Twayne's World Authors Series No. 862

G. W. F. Hegel
Howard P. Kainz

Twayne Publishers
An Imprint of Simon & Schuster Macmillan
1633 Broadway
New York, New York 10019

Library of Congress Cataloging-in-Publication Data
Kainz, Howard P.
    G.W.F. Hegel / Howard P. Kainz.
        p.   cm. — (Twayne's world author's series ; TWAS 862)
    Includes bibliographical references and index.
    ISBN 0-8057-7808-X (cloth : alk. paper)
    1. Hegel, Georg Wilhelm Friedrich, 1770–1831. I. Title.
  II. Series.
  B2948.K24   1996
  193—dc20   96-38516
                                                    CIP

10 9 8 7 6 5 4 3 2 1

To my parents

Contents

Publisher's Note

Twayne's first volume on *G. W. F. Hegel,* by Clark Butler, appeared in 1977. In recognition of recent advances in Hegel scholarship, we are pleased to offer this new critical study of nineteenth-century Germany's foremost philosopher.

Preface

I. Hegel's System, Prima Facie

Imagine the situation of someone who is familiar with the history of philosophy but is now for the first time confronting Hegel's system— let's say, the condensed version of the later system in the *Encyclopedia of Philosophical Sciences.* He or she browses through the pages and notices the arrangement of topics: being, quantity, essence, space, time, chemistry, consciousness, the state, history, art, religion, philosophy, etc.— all concatenated, each apparently in a deductive relationship to what precedes it.

First, one wonders what category or genre to put this work into. Aristotle's great attempt to encompass all extant fields of knowledge in a scientific framework comes to mind, and perhaps Spinoza's attempt to construct a system based on orderly inferences *in ordine geometrico,* and possibly other attempts at building grand systems.

But then one wonders whether such systems are grand or just grandiose. If they are grand, then we may admire the ambition and dedication of talented people in the past who tried to encompass all existing knowledge in a philosophical system that would mirror the system of the world—although of course we need to add that such an enterprise would be impossible for even the greatest genius in our own day, when an ongoing "knowledge explosion" is splintering knowledge into thousands of specializations and subspecializations. On the other hand, if a system like this is merely grandiose, then we may react with astonishment at the hubris—and the cheek—of anyone, even the most gifted, who would aspire to such a peak of knowledge. We might see such a creation as an inflated balloon, and we might be tempted to puncture a few holes in it, thus serving the cause of humanity, which has been ill-served by idle, ivory-tower philosophical speculation.

In the case of Hegel's system, the choice between these two evaluations is not easy. Hegel offers so much that is valuable and immensely insightful that even his enemies and critics—Kierkegaard, Marx, Sartre, and others—have ended up borrowing from him. But anyone who studies Hegel also comes across hairsplitting sophistries, non sequiturs, bad science, chauvinism, and prejudices. If "throwing out the baby with the bathwater" is to be avoided, a thorough examination of this complex system is in order. It is my contention that such an examination is worthwhile and necessary, and that it will lead us to something like a middle ground between "grand" and "grandiose."

Some books on Hegel's system, or on parts of his system, have proceeded paragraph by paragraph or section by section. Having benefited from such treatments, I will try to supplement the efforts of other authors by concentrating on overall structures and features, and on the background and high points—as one might proceed in trying to describe a cathedral. Finally, I will attempt to distinguish between what is viable and important and what is outdated or insignificant in Hegel's system, from our vantage point at the end of the twentieth century.

II. G. W. F. Hegel (1770–1831): Biographical Notes

Hegel at age thirty-four summed up the milestones in his life in a narrative-form curriculum vitae, written when he was applying for a teaching position at the University of Jena:

I, Ge[org] W[ilhelm] Fr[iedrich] H[egel], [was] born in Stuttgart on the 27th of August, 1770. My parents, G[eorg] L[udwig] Hegel, an expeditionary councilor for the Board of Revenue and Ch[ristine] L[uise] [Hegel], née Fromm, provided for my education in the sciences both through private tutoring and through public instruction at the *Gymnasium* in Stuttgart, where ancient and modern languages as well as basic principles of the sciences were taught. I was accepted at age eighteen in the Theological Institute at Tübingen. After two years, spent in the study of philology under Schn[urrer] and the study of philosophy and mathematics under Flatt and Beckh, I received a Master's degree in philosophy, and then studied the theological sciences three years under Le Bret, Uhland, Storr and Flatt, until I passed the theological examination before the Consistory in Stuttgart and was accepted as a candidate in theology. I had entered into the profession of preaching according to the wish of my parents, and I had remained steadfast in my study of theology on account of its connection with classical literature and philosophy. After I was admitted, I chose from among the occupational specializations in theology positions that, being independent of the tasks peculiar to the profession (the vocation of preacher), offered me the leisure to devote myself to ancient literature and philosophy, while at the same time affording the opportu-

nity of living in a foreign environment in other countries. I found such
conditions in the two tutoring positions which I accepted in Bern and in
Frankfurt; the duties connected with these positions left me enough time
to proceed on the path of science that I had made my life's objective. After
the six years that I spent in these two positions, and after the death of my
father, I decided to dedicate myself completely to philosophical science;
and the reputation of the University of Jena left me no other choice concerning the place where I could find the opportunity not only to continue
in the finest manner with the projects I had been working on, but also to
try out the teaching profession. I wrote an essay there on the difference
between Fichte's and Schelling's system of philosophy—the former
[Fichte's] being an unsatisfactory system—and I then obtained my license
for teaching from the officials by means of the public defense of my dissertation, *On the Orbits of the Planets.* Along with Professor Schelling I edited
two issues of the *Critical Journal of Philosophy.* My own contributions were
as follows:

> The Introduction,
> How the ordinary human understanding encounters philosophy,
> On ancient and modern skepticism,
> Kantian, Jacobian, and Fichtean philosophy,
> Recent work on natural law.

As a Privatdozent in philosophy for the last three years, I have given a
variety of lectures on philosophy, and last winter, I would say, to a siz-
able audience. The Ducal Mineralogical Society admitted me as the second Assessor during the previous year; the Natural Science Society
recently accepted me as a member.

Thus insofar as the science of philosophy has become my calling under
so many aspects, I cannot help but hope to be appointed as a public lecturer in philosophy by the distinguished authorities.[1]

If we examine Hegel's references here to his seminary years and his
studies of theology—"according to the wish of my parents," "on account
of its connection with classical literature and philosophy," "being independent of the tasks peculiar to the profession, the vocation of
preacher"—we notice definite indications that Hegel was leaving theology behind, that his study had not been completely voluntary, that his
first love had always been philosophy.

Hegel began his training as a Lutheran clergyman in the seminary at
Tübingen in 1788. His classmates and eventual roommates included the

future poet Friedrich Hölderlin and the future philosopher Friedrich
Schelling. His studies were in philosophy and theology; and, as he indicates in his vita, he began to experience a conflict between these two
interests. He also cultivated his social life intensively in the seminary
years, becoming noteworthy for frequenting local taverns and partici-
pating in games, including kissing games.

In philosophy, the young Hegel seemed more interested in political
philosophy than metaphysics. Kant was the rage at the time (Kant's
Critique of Pure Reason and *Critique of Practical Reason* had just recently
been published); but when Hegel was offered membership in the campus Kant Club, he declined, replying that he was too busy studying
Rousseau.

The political philosophy of Jean-Jacques Rousseau had indeed captured
the imagination of France and much of Europe. On the Tübingen campus,
a Political Club focused primarily on Rousseau's republicanism was formed.
Hegel did not join it, but possibly he did accompany some friends, sympathetic to the French Revolution, in a demonstration in which a "liberty
tree" was erected in memory of its ideals.[2] As the French Revolution turned
ugly and self-destructive, Hegel shared the disappointment of his friends;
and eventually, like many others in Germany, came to look to Napoléon as
a better, more stable exemplar of the spirit of freedom.

Hegel received his master's degree in philosophy at Tübingen in
1790 with a rather low final ranking ("fourth in a class of five"). There
did seem to be some bias against Hegel, possibly because of his drinking
habits (once, in a drunken stupor, he had to be smuggled into the seminary after hours by his roommates) and his frequent fines and demerits
for infractions of the rules. Another reason for the faculty's irritation
may have been the fact that Hegel (always an admirer of the Greeks,
and upset about the melancholy nature of Christian rituals) had joined
with comrades in offering sacrifices to Bacchus at some of their gather-
ings. However, on Hegel's seminary certificate, his tutors did note that
he had "put much effort into the study of philosophy" (*"philosophiae mul-
tam operam impendit"*). After Hegel's death, Eduard Zeller, in an essay on
Hegel in the *Theologische Jahrbücher* in 1845, deliberately changed *"mul-
tam"* ("much") to *"nullam"* ("not any") (Wiedmann 23); later, Rudolf
Haym, in his major biography of Hegel—*Hegel und seine Zeit*—simply
retained Zeller's version, giving rise, in some quarters, to the legend
that Hegel was backward in philosophy.

Hegel did have real problems with preaching, however. His practice
sermons at the seminary did not produce any breakthrough; and he did

not pursue a position in the Lutheran ministry after graduation. Instead, like many graduates at that time, he took a "stepping-stone" job as a tutor. His first position (1793–1796) was with the Steiger von Tschugg family in Berne, Switzerland. His tutoring work with the four children in the family left him ample time to read Grotius, Hobbes, Hume, Leibniz, Locke, Montesquieu, Shaftsbury, Spinoza, Voltaire, Kant, and Fichte. Hegel had apparently acquired a knowledge of English by this time. During his second tutoring position (1797–1800)—with the Gogel family in Frankfurt, Germany—Hegel sketched out what Nohl would later title "A Fragment of a System."[3]

Hegel left his position in Frankfurt after receiving a small inheritance when his father died in 1799; he then moved to Jena, where he lived with his friend Schelling, who was a professor at the University of Jena, and began teaching as an unsalaried university lecturer at the university. During this period he published *The Difference between Fichte's and Schelling's System of Philosophy,* a generally sympathetic assessment of Schelling's response to Johann Fichte's revision of Kantianism. He also coedited a philosophical journal, *The Critical Journal of Philosophy,* with Schelling, until Schelling left for a position at the University of Würtzburg in 1803. In 1805, Hegel was appointed an associate professor at Jena. Serious differences in ideas and methodology had been developing between him and Schelling during this period, and these came out subtly but unmistakably in Hegel's first book, *The Phenomenology of Spirit,* completed on the eve of the battle of Jena. After that, his relations with Schelling were rare and strained.

Hegel fled Jena as Napoléon entered the city victoriously after the battle of Jena. As a result of the war, the University of Jena was closed; this dampened Hegel's hopes of a professorship there; and subsequently, with the help of his best friend, Friedrich Niethammer, he obtained a job as a newspaper editor with the *Bamburger Zeitung.* In 1808, he took a position as instructor and headmaster at a high school (*Gymnasium*) in Nürnberg.

In 1811, Hegel married Marie von Tucher. Their daughter, Susanna Hegel, was born in 1812, but she died shortly after birth; Karl Hegel was born in 1813 and Immanuel Hegel in 1814. Having published a major two-volume work, *The Science of Logic,* between 1812 and 1816, Hegel was offered a professorship at the University of Heidelberg in 1816 and accepted it.

In 1817, the year of the publication of the first edition of his *Encyclopedia of Philosophical Sciences,* Hegel and his wife brought into their family

Hegel's illegitimate son, Ludwig, who had been born in 1807. Ludwig had great difficulty fitting in with Hegel's legitimate family, and when he was accused of petty theft during his apprenticeship to a merchant, Hegel forced him to take his mother's family name, Fischer. Ludwig joined the Dutch colonial army in 1825 and died of a fever in India in 1831.

In 1818, Hegel accepted a professorship at the University of Berlin, where he very soon became an object of jealousy for the proud philosopher Arthur Schopenhauer ("posterity will set up a monument to me"). Schopenhauer scheduled his lectures to coincide with Hegel's but unfortunately lost this popularity contest. Hegel, though he had no remarkable oratorical skills, gained great popularity in Germany. On the occasion of his fifty-sixth birthday in 1826, the university organized a grand-scale twenty-four-hour joint birthday party for him and his friend, Goethe. However, Hegel was less popular with Catholics than with Protestants. When a Catholic student complained in 1826 about Hegel's tirades against Catholic doctrines (such as transubstantiation in the eucharist), there was an official inquiry, to which Hegel replied that he was Lutheran, always would be a Lutheran, and was teaching in a Protestant university, and that a Catholic student at the University of Berlin should not be surprised at being in critical Lutheran hands. Still, the Catholic Church as a whole never officially considered Hegel's teachings pernicious. For example, although Kant's *Critique of Pure Reason* was placed on the Vatican's *Index of Forbidden Books,* none of Hegel's writings appeared in it.

In 1829—by chance, and for the last time—Hegel met his former friend Schelling at the baths at Karlsbad. They spent time in conversation, and both sent written reports to their wives about the encounter. Hegel, in a surprised tone, portrayed it as very amicable. Schelling, on the other hand, smarting from Hegel's public criticism of his philosophy, told his wife that they had managed to avoid friction by abstaining from any "scientific" subjects (Althaus 571–72). That same year, Hegel, at the peak of his popularity, was elected president of the University of Berlin.

Hegel's death in 1831 was officially ascribed to cholera; but the actual cause seems to have been a chronic stomach ailment—probably aggravated by an irritating popularity contest between Hegel and his former pupil Eduard Gans, now lecturing at Berlin on philosophy of law and drawing students away from Hegel's course on the same subject

(Wiedmann 108, Althaus 579–81). Hegel was buried, as he had wished, next to the philosopher Fichte.

Shortly after Hegel's death, the *Halle Yearbook*, a Hegelian review, began publication; articles in the *Yearbook* by Feuerbach and Marx led to communism. However, Kierkegaard's existentialist reaction against Hegel began about the same time. And conflicts between the "left" and "right" Hegelians, and "old" and "young" Hegelians—which still persist—also began in full force.

Acknowledgments

I am grateful to Professor Andreas Arndt, editor of the *Hegel Jahrbuch,* for permission to use parts of my papers "Hegel, Democracy, and the 'Kingdom of God,'" published in 1994; and "Hegel, Providence, and the Philosophy of History," published in 1996. I am also grateful to Professor Lawrence Stepelevich, editor of *The Owl of Minerva,* for permission to use part of my article "What Is Living and What Is Dead in Hegel, Today?" published in June 1979.

Chronology

1770   Georg Wilhelm Friedrich Hegel born August 27 in Stuttgart, Germany, the first son of Georg Ludwig Hegel and Maria Magdalena Hegel.

1788   Enters Tübingen Seminary. Eventually shares room with Friedrich Hölderlin and Friedrich Schelling.

1790   Receives master of philosophy degree.

1793   Passes consistorial examination in theology. Takes position as tutor in Berne, Switzerland. Continues studies in philosophy.

1797   Takes new tutoring position in Frankfurt. Drafts a plan for a system of philosophy—*A Fragment of a System.*

1801   Moves to Jena, defends dissertation, receives *Habilitation,* thus qualifying for professorship, begins teaching as Privatdozent at University of Jena.

1805   Appointed associate professor of Philosophy at Jena.

1806   Flees Jena on invasion of Napoléon.

1807   *The Phenomenology of Spirit.* Hegel takes position as editor of the *Bamberg News.*

1808   Takes position as instructor and administrator in a *Gymnasium* in Nürnberg.

1811   Marries Marie von Tucher.

1812–1816   Multivolume *Science of Logic.*

1816   Takes position as professor of philosophy at University of Heidelberg.

1817   *Encyclopedia of Philosophical Sciences,* first edition.

1818   Takes position as professor at University of Berlin.

1821   *Philosophy of Right.*

1827   Second edition of the *Encyclopedia.*

1829   Appointed president of the University of Berlin.

1830   Third edition of the *Encyclopedia.*

1831   Dies of cholera, November 14.

Abbreviations

Chapter One
Characteristics of Hegel's System

I. Dialectic

"Dialectic" has acquired multiple, often conflicting, meanings in the history of western philosophy. It has been identified with rhetoric, sophistry, Socratic "cross-examination," Platonic ascent from the sensible to the spiritual, late-Platonic definition by division into genera and species, Aristotelian sifting of opinions pro and con, Kantian "transcendental" illusions of the understanding, Marxian socioeconomic stages through capitalism to socialism, etc.

Hegel's name is often connected with dialectic, but Hegel takes pains to distinguish his philosophical approach from a sophistic or merely rhetorical use of dialectic:

> Dialectic is usually characterized as a superficial ingenuity for arbitrarily injecting confusion and a mere semblance of contradictions into determinate concepts, so that this semblance of contradictions (not the resultant determinations) is viewed as a nullity, standing in stark contrast with the intelligible "truth."[1]

For Hegel, on the other hand, dialectic is not something externally induced but the soul of determinate concepts, resulting from the very fact that they are finite and situated in a context of otherness:

> Dialectic is the immanent forthgoing wherein the onesidedness and limitedness of intellectual determinations shows itself for what it is— namely, the negation of these same determinations (H1, §15).

Hegel is here echoing Spinoza's maxim "Every determination is a negation"—that is, determinations lead to their opposites—but he goes further than Spinoza. Hegel observes that the determinate negations themselves generate "dialectical" relationships to other determinations, outside the parameters of the initial finite determinations. As we explore a specific determination, we arrive at its limits and are necessarily drawn into a consideration of that which it negates, that which is other, and

1

especially that which is diametrically other: the opposite to which it is
conceptually related. Then the process continues. This analysis of determinations in terms of their essential negative relationship to other determinations is the dialectical element fundamental to Hegel's philosophizing, and it prevails throughout his system.

II. Speculation

Dialectic as a generation of oppositions—even necessary, diametrical
oppositions—could turn out to be an infinite seesaw, leading nowhere.
Thus it is important to understand that in Hegel's system, dialectic is
methodically subordinated to "speculation." Hegel frequently used ordinary words in their etymological sense; "speculation" is related to the
Latin *speculatio,* which was used by late Roman philosophers to signify
philosophical contemplation of ultimate realities. Speculation, in the
Hegelian sense, takes up just where dialectic—in the negative, pejorative sense of the "Transcendental Dialectic" in Kant's *Critique of Pure
Reason*—leaves off:

> If we remain fastened on just the abstract, negative aspect, contributed
> by dialectic, the outcome is just the familiar [Kantian] position that Rea-
> son is "incapable of knowing the infinite." This is a peculiar outcome, in
> view of the fact that the infinite *is* the rational. . . . The Speculative con-
> sists in the dialectic as it is here elaborated, *and* simultaneously in the
> grasping of the unity, i.e. of the positive within the negative.[2]

This is a special characteristic of Hegel's system: developing dialectical negations in detail, but then—without losing sight of, or doing away
with, the opposition—bringing them into "unity in difference."
Throughout the three parts of Hegel's system, there are many instances
of this speculative "moment," which grasps the positive amid the negative, but a few examples will help to elucidate its nature.

For one example, in the concluding parts of Logic, the "Idea" (in
Hegel's special, technical sense) is a final conceptual development hold-
ing together numerous oppositions that have already been treated in
earlier parts:

> The Idea can be grasped as . . . the subject-object, as the unity of the
> ideal and the real, of the finite and the infinite, of the soul and the body;
> as the possibility that contains its actuality in itself, and thus as that
> whose nature can be conceptualized only as existing.[3]

For a second example, in Philosophy of Nature, Hegel points to polarity as a concrete manifestation of the speculative "Idea" in phenomenal reality, and to magnetism—a unifying force which divides itself into north and south polarity—as one of the best examples of the speculative grasping-together of opposites:

> If someone suggests that thought is not present in nature, we can show him thought here [in the form of magnetism]. . . . What is identical in both poles presents itself as different; and what is different in both of them presents itself as identical (E2, §§312, 314).

Numerous additional examples of dialectical-speculative "unity in difference" can be found in the last part of the *Encyclopedia,* Philosophy of Spirit. Sense-consciousness, which gets into a dialectic when it tries unsuccessfully to focus on the "here" and the "now" as isolated, particular sensations, offers an especially good example:

> The content of sensory consciousness is itself intrinsically dialectical. The content ought to be *the* particular here or now; but at the very same time it is not *one* particular, but every particular here or now; and just as soon as the particular content excludes an "other" from itself, it immediately also relates itself to the other, and gives evidence that it is *transcending itself,* that it is dependent on the other, that it is mediated through the other, that it itself has the other in itself (EIII, §419, Zusatz).

The speculative philosopher, in Hegel's estimation, is not caught up in one-sided determinate viewpoints and is able to avoid endless juggling of dialectical oppositions for their own sake. Speculative philosophers can engage in a complex type of contemplation which clearly sees and presents an opposition that emerges into unity but is not dissolved or nullified in that unity.

III. Science

After one has read Hegel extensively, there is no missing his message: Hegel claims, in hundreds of places in his writings, that philosophy must be a science, and he claims to be constructing a scientific philosophical system. This causes a strange clang in the ears of English-speakers, who have come to associate the word "science," narrowly, with the empirical sciences. German-speakers may have an easier time accepting this idea, since they make a distinction between the natural sciences (*Naturwis-*

senschaften) and the human sciences or humanities (*Geisteswissenschaften*)—although that distinction did not exist in Hegel's time.

In his use of the term "science"—with "system" as a synonym—Hegel is harking back to Aristotle's idea of science as a body of knowledge organized through necessary causes, in contrast to collections of opinions laden with contingencies. Aristotle's distinction between "dialectic" and "science" (*episteme*) parallels Plato's distinction between the "upward path" of dialectical progression to the ultimate Ideas and the "downward path" of the philosopher's reversion to the world to apply the Ideas or Forms to sensible reality. Science for Aristotle is also a downward path: the philosopher, after arriving at self-evident principles through induction and dialectic, uses syllogistic reasoning and deduction to construct an *organically interconnected* body of ideas. Hegel insists that philosophy must be scientific, in a similar sense, when he speaks somewhat metaphorically about the way in which progress through philosophical subject matter must be conducted:

> The movement of the pure essentialities is what constitutes the nature of science. Considered as the interconnection of the contents of science, this movement is its necessity and its elaboration into the organic totality. . . . Scientific knowledge requires a subordination to the life of the object; or, in other words, giving precedence to the inner necessity of the object and bringing out this necessity.[4]

The scientific concatenation of "essentialities" which Hegel has in mind is intended also to have an effect on the natural sciences, since

> though philosophy is commonly held to be a formal, content-less type of knowledge, . . . nevertheless, whatever as regards content in any other kind of knowledge and science is "truth," can be worthy of this name only if it has been begotten from philosophy. . . . As regards the other sciences, let them pursue truth as much as they want with ratiocination, they will not be able without philosophy to embody life, spirit, truth (PS, 46).

Hegel's concept of the relationship of philosophy to the empirical sciences is discussed in detail later, in Chapter 6.

IV. Emphasis on the Subject-Object Problematic

Even someone with a sophisticated background in philosophy, seeing the above heading, might react by asking, "*What* subject-object problematic?" But certainly something on the order of a subject-object problematic has developed in twentieth-century quantum physics, with Werner Heisenberg's principle of indeterminacy and the "Copenhagen interpretation" of microcosmic events. According to Heisenberg's principle, subjective factors and subjectively chosen instrumentation must be taken into account in a physicist's judgments about the position or momentum of subatomic particles. According to the Copenhagen interpretation, the complete inseparability of subjective and objective factors is simply more noticeable in microphysics but is in principle also applicable to macrophysical phenomena. If this is true, one might expect philosophy, especially metaphysics and epistemology, to be developing in the direction of overcoming subject-object indeterminacy or uncertainty. But in contemporary philosophy one has to look long and hard to find books or articles devoted to any "subject-object problematic." One relatively recent, and very successful, exception is Rorty's *Philosophy and the Mirror of Nature,*[5] a full-scale examination of the dualistic impasse resulting from Cartesian-foundationalist epistemology. Rorty's rather tentative solution for "overcoming epistemology" (which appears toward the end of his book) is a new focus on "conversation" in philosophy. His models for "conversation" include John Dewey, and Wittgenstein and Heidegger in their later years—a diverse group of philosophers with very different perspectives. Rorty believes that these models have in common the linguistic-hermeneutic task of showing how to bridge the gaps between varying types of discourse.

In Hegel's estimation, Cartesian dualism is just one offshoot of the pivotal and perennial philosophical problem, the relationship of subject to object:

> The relation of concept to being, or subject to object, confronts us right up to the most recent times with one of the most interesting issues—or better, *the* most interesting, albeit also the most difficult issue—in philosophy, which has not yet arrived at elucidation (E1, §139).

Hegel's interest in this problem was shared by F. W. J. Schelling, who, following initial efforts by Fichte, devised a system constructed around an absolute "Subject-Object."[6] This is the endeavor that signalized German idealism at the onset of the nineteenth century, an endeavor calculated to overcome the Kantian impasse of a "thing in itself" construed dualistically as existing objectively—outside the understanding and forever just beyond the grasp of the understanding.

This was a dichotomy waiting to be abolished, and Hegel enthusiastically took up the challenge of abolishing it. In one place, he compares overcoming the contradiction between subject and object to the Christian symbolism of atonement after the fall of Adam and Eve from their state of original innocence and the consequent divorce, through sin, of nature from spirit (HP2, 246).

Fichte (before Hegel) and Schelling (at the same time as Hegel) were also concerned with overcoming dualism. But Hegel believed that Fichte had ended up with a subjectively tainted presentation of the original unity—Hegel's code name for this is "subjective subject-object"—and that Schelling had been similarly unsuccessful when he arbitrarily asserted a nonsubjective "absolute point of indifference of subject and object." Hegel's own strategy was to prepare the way for acceptance of an absolute subject-object (which he code-named the "Idea") in and through an elaborate quasi-inductive process in his *Phenomenology of Spirit*.[7] Hegel outlines this strategy in the Introduction to *Phenomenology* and gradually works toward the presentation of this absolute.

Stages along the way in the *Phenomenology* include the second chapter, "Perception," which analyzes the perceptual object as a meeting ground of objective qualities and subjective predications (this is something like a complex variation of Locke's primary and secondary qualities); and, in the fourth chapter, the "Stoical consciousness," a type of subjectivity which finds objectivity within itself and creates its own objective determinations. Toward the middle of the *Phenomenology,* in the chapter titled "Reason," Hegel gives us a rather clear idea of the new sort of philosophical category he has in mind. He contrasts Aristotle's overly objective ten categories with Kant's overly subjective twelve categories; and he speaks about a new Category of Reason, expressing the unity of consciousness with all reality (Kainz 1976, 98–99). As the phenomenology of Reason evolves into the phenomenology of Spirit, the subjective-objective Category becomes more finely tuned. An almost untranslatable configuration appears, *die Sache selbst*—the "really real"?—a subjective-objective individuality that takes itself as its own objective "task," and in this way both finds and makes itself in expressing itself. A little further along the way, in the long sixth chapter, "Spirit," a form of the world appears on the horizon: the "Ethical Substance," a type of social system (after the Greek pattern) in which each subjectivity finds its meaning in the whole social objectivity, and the whole expresses the subjectivities that make it up. Some more sophisticated appearances of the subject-object include "conscientiousness," at the end of the sixth chapter ("Spirit"), a type of consciousness fully in tune with objective reality, including its own feeling; and, in the seventh chapter, "Revealed Religion," the ultimate religion (Christianity), in which the divine subjectivity becomes fully objectified in the incarnation of a God-man. In the last chapter, the stage of "Absolute Knowledge," initially adumbrated in the introduction to the *Phenomenology,* finally emerges. This is a type of knowledge which brings together the highest subjective "scientific" methodology (Fichte's analysis of ego and non-ego) and the highest objective content (the objective expressions of divine subjectivity in the Christian religion). What is the *object* of Absolute Knowledge? One could say that the finally emerging subjective-objective Category becomes the proper "object" of "Absolute Knowledge" in this final chapter; but strictly, the word "object" is no longer relevant or applicable at this juncture, since the entire thrust of the *Phenomenology* is to overcome, in its conclusion, the rift between knowledge and object of knowledge.

In Hegel's later system, all of the categorial developments are meant to be "rational realities"—manifestations of a unique *sui generis* Concept fully permeated with existence. Hegel refers, as a model, to St. Anselm's proof of the existence of God; Anselm argued that there is a certain unique type of concept which necessarily includes real existence. It is the development of this concept-object that Hegel is concerned with. This single, unique Concept can also be presented as a single, unique Object—the World, or God as Absolute Object, breaking up into distinct objects (as the Concept breaks up into distinct concepts), manifesting various "unities in distinction" (E1, §193). According to Hegel, the only way in which he differs from Anselm is that in his own philosophical system it will be necessary to go beyond Anselm's positive insight about the conceptual unity of being and thought, and to develop the negativity or the negative interrelationships concomitant to that unity (H1, §139).

The absolute subjective-objective Category reached in the *Phenomenology of Spirit* becomes the starting point of Hegel's later system, where the emphasis is more specifically on thought-being rather than on subject-object. In the course of the later system, the initial abstract subjective-objective Category takes on more and more concrete expressions. In the Logic, the Category appears as an initial "unity in difference" between being and nothingness, and then, as a kind of self-moving and self-propagating principle, widens into quality-quantity, essence-existence; it reaches its final explicit formulation when it becomes the Idea (Logos). The Idea subsequently needs external expression, and its further unfolding supplies the transition to Hegel's Philosophy of Nature. There, the unity of being and thought is manifested in space-time, in electric and magnetic polarity, etc.; but it reaches its highest point in the organism, in which the objectivity of matter becomes permeated with the subjectivity of life. This final stage in the Philosophy of Nature then leads to the Philosophy of Spirit, and the ultimate "concrete" developments of subjective-objective "unity in difference"—the psyche, the family, civil society, the state, and finally "Absolute Spirit" (art, religion, and philosophy), in which the highest reaches of subjectivity are expressed externally in culture.

V. Circularity

Circularity is usually thought of as a problem in logic and philosophy, as well as in grammar. The classical "fallacy" *circulus vitiosus*—"vicious circle"—is a good illustration of problematic circularity. In order to avoid this fallacy, one must conscientiously avoid using a defined word in its definition, or presupposing something that is to be proved in an argument, or setting up an airtight philosophical system which needs to prove its own validity. Circularity becomes even more "vicious" as we produce statements or ideas which combine circularity with contradiction, as in "The statement I am making now is false" or in the argument that a true skeptic would have to be skeptical about his or her skepticism, and hence would not be a skeptic. What happens in such cases is that we stretch language and grammar to its limits, almost trying to make it bend back on itself, recapture itself, and sometimes even catch itself in a contradiction. The predictable result is that the mind, like a computer receiving a command which puts it into a recursive "loop," finds itself spinning but getting nowhere.

But if language cannot circle back on itself and recapture itself, possibly self-consciousness *can* do this. Possibly, it is the experience of self-consciousness that has led some hardy logicians to try to get language to mimic this circular movement. And if self-consciousness can, as the term seems to imply, be aware of its awareness, or think about its thinking, a certain type of infinite circular motion results, in which subject is transformed into object and vice versa, until consciousness steps out from this intense interior activity into more straightforward cognitive endeavors. In Hegel's estimation, *this* circularity is true infinity—not the specious type of infinity which results from successively setting finite boundaries and then negating them, as happens in mathematical operations.

During his Frankfurt period (1797–1801), Hegel considered philosophy subordinate to religion, precisely because religion embodied true infinity. The prime locus of this embodiment was the Christian doctrine of the Trinity: an infinite, eternal circular relationship of three divine persons proceeding from each other. Hegel thought then that philosophy, having to do with finite determinations, could rise to the infinite only through collaboration with religion. But in his Jena period (1801–1807), he began to see a possibility of incorporating infinity within philosophy itself. In *The Difference between Fichte's and Schelling's System of Philosophy,* Hegel anticipated some contemporary "nonfoundationalist" epistemological approaches by proposing a "self-grounding" system of philosophy which would avoid a question-begging—counterproductive, unidirectional linear dependence of conclusions on grounds or first principles:

> While philosophy in itself as a totality grounds itself, and likewise the reality of knowledge, in terms of form and content, the [post-Kantian] thrust towards foundationalism and grounding, in contrast, with all its marshalling of justifications and analyses, and with all its usage of "whereas" and "to the extent that" and "therefore" and "insofar," neither gets outside itself nor enters into philosophy. . . . [In contrast, philosophical] Science claims to be *self*-grounding, insofar as it establishes each of its parts absolutely and in doing so constitutes identity and knowledge at the beginning and in each particular point. As objective totality knowledge grounds itself even more, the more it is elaborated; and its parts are just at the same time grounded with this totality of knowledge. The middle-point and periphery are related to each other in such a way that the very beginning of the circle is already a relationship to the middle-point, and the latter is not a full-fledged middle-point unless the whole circle of its relationships is completed.[8]

As in the doctrine of the Trinity, the "infinite" circularity intrinsic to philosophy will be connected with triads or triplicity. Hegel rarely uses the terminology "thesis-antithesis-synthesis," but his works are full of methodological movements from position to counterposition to a higher position which incorporates (*aufhebt*) both opposites. The geometrical contrast between triangle and circle may be an obstacle in this case; but with a little imagination, it becomes clear that triangularity merges into circularity. Since Hegel himself uses geometrical analogies to describe the structure of his system, I may be excused for using diagrams to illustrate the merger in question. In Figure 1, the multiple layers of arcs gradually merge into a full-fledged circle; and, as Figure 2 illustrates, interconnected triads can also lead into an interconnected circularity.

Donald Verene, in *Hegel's Recollection*,[9] no doubt in the interest of defending Hegel from pedantry and formalism, makes the astounding statement that there is no triplicity in Hegel. This assertion is based on a misunderstanding of a reference to triplicity in the Preface to Hegel's *Phenomenology of Spirit*. Hegel does (PS, 37) criticize Kant's abstract, formalistic use of triplicity; but he asserts that now it has been raised to the level of an absolute method. Verene is incorrect in saying that there are only two places where Hegel speaks of triadic thought. (See, for example, E1, §171, Zusatz; §215, Zusatz; §230, Zusatz; E2, §248, Zusatz; §255; and §270, Zusatz.) One must let Hegel be Hegel. There are literally thousands of triads in Hegel's system of philosophy; Hegel speaks often of triplicity, and the triplicity is interrelated with circularity. Likewise, the ultimate circularity of the system as a whole is a consequence of its triplicity. A detailed examination of the interrelation of the three parts of the system is undertaken later, in chapter three.

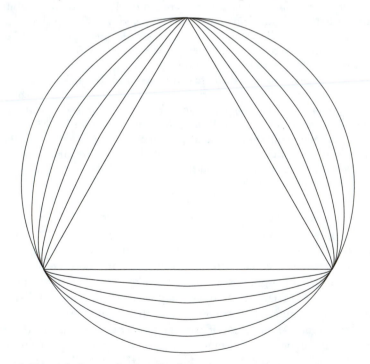

Figure 1. Triangularity merging into circularity.

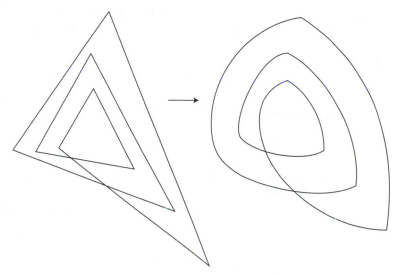

Figure 2. Interconnected triads portrayed as interconnected circularity.

VI. Paradox

The term "paradox" has been used to encompass many things that are not paradoxical in the strict sense. For example, a popular computer software database program, Paradox, includes the following lines from Gilbert and Sullivan's *The Pirates of Penzance* in the frontispiece to one of its manuals:

Frederic: A paradox?
King: A paradox!
Ruth: A most ingenious paradox!
   We've quips and quibbles heard in flocks,
    But none to beat this paradox! . . .
Frederic: How quaint the ways of paradox!
Ruth, King: A paradox, a paradox,
   A most ingenious paradox.

The "paradox" in this case is that Frederic was born in a leap year, and thus has had only five birthdays, even though he is turning twenty-one—a paradox only in the sense that it is a remarkable fact, contrary to the expectations of Frederic, a slave who has not known the details of his birth.

In another Paradox manual, the frontispiece, with a little more accuracy, cites the physicist Niels Bohr, referring to the "paradoxes" of quantum mechanics: "How wonderful that we have met with paradox. Now we have some hope of making progress." This is closer to "paradox" in the strict sense, but still only an approximation.

An oxymoron like "loud silence" or "lonely crowd" is, of course, just a shortened form of paradox. For some strange reason, "oxymoron" in common parlance has come to signify a contradiction in terms. But, like paradox, it is not a contradiction.

A paradox, in the primary and most important meaning, is an *apparent* contradiction; to repeat, the contradiction is only apparent, and indeed it expresses a profound truth. The so-called "logical paradoxes" (the Cretan who says that it is true that all Cretans are liars, and so forth) and the "paradoxes" of quantum physics (e.g., the fact that a moving particle with a definite momentum has no definite position) do not fit this description. They are, rather, only apparent paradoxes that either contain real contradictions (as the "liar" paradox does) or go against the expectations of observers (as do the paradoxes of quantum physics).

Paradox in religion depends on a belief system. (Examples include the Christian paradoxes "The last shall be first, and the first last" and "He who saves his life will lose it, but he who loses his life for my sake will save it"). Paradox in literature—for example, the poems of metaphysical poets like John Donne and Restoration poets like William Congreve— appeals especially to aesthetic intuition, unless it begins to merge with philosophical argumentation, as in the writings of G. K. Chesterton. The distinguishing feature of paradox in philosophy is that it is independent of any religious belief system and relies on rational argumentation rather than aesthetic appeal. What it has in common with other forms of paradox is an attempt to bring opposites together: the greater the oppositions that are coordinated, the greater the paradox.

What greater opposition can there be than that between subject and object? The subject-object opposition is prior to, and a necessary presupposition for, all the oppositions that can be discerned in the objective sphere or in the realm of ideas. Drawing up a unity between these two archetypal opposites, and all their ramifications, would be an essentially paradoxical enterprise. And this is precisely what Hegel attempts to do in his system.

According to Hegel, the paradoxical unity of subject and object is not just an abstract theory; it has a basis in the experience of self-consciousness. In the Introduction to his *Phenomenology,* (PS, 64–66), Hegel asks us to recall what happens when consciousness takes itself as an object—when it becomes conscious of its own consciousness. In such a case, the distinction between "concept" and "object" vanishes; the concept that we form is also the object that we are conceptualizing, and we would get into an epistemological impasse if we tried to answer the question: Does the concept conform to the object, or vice versa? In like manner, in any second-order object—e.g., my hierarchy of values taken as my object of reflection—the conventional distinction between subject and object becomes impossible to maintain.

The categories in Hegel's system are multiple manifestations of the paradoxical unity of subject and object. In the history of western philosophy, according to Hegel, the paradigmatic example of subjectivity-objectivity is the concept of Being. Parmenides' statement that "it is the same thing that can be and can be thought"[10] set the stage for innumerable philosophical variations on the theme of subject-object unity, up to the modern era. But the most concrete examples (in Hegel's sense of "concrete," which is synonymous with "spiritually complex") of the paradoxical unity of being and thought are to be found in the "philosophy of Spirit," where we deal with fusions of consciousness and existence in the state, and in art, religion, and philosophy itself.

VII. A Dialectical System

At first glance, it seems that a dialectical system would be not just a paradox, but a contradiction in terms. "Dialectic," after all, connotes oscillation between opposites—opposite subjective viewpoints or opposite objective determinations—and "system" in the strict Hegelian sense, as adumbrated above, connotes a presentation of the absolute subjective-objective Idea as a *unity* in all its manifestations. Thus, in the face of continuing references to Hegel as a "dialectician," some clarifications and qualifications need to be made.

If we take "dialectic" as implying oscillation between opposing viewpoints—the sort of approach that characterizes Platonic dialogues and other classical philosophical dialogues, such as Hume's *Dialogues on Natural Religion* and Berkeley's *Three Dialogues between Hylas And Philonous*—dialectic seems to run counter to the intent of systematization. It would seem, at the very least, that such dialectical endeavors could be no more than systems with a small "s," since systematization is clearly subordinated to dialectic. But Hegel's work is characterized by constant coordination of dialectic and system, rather than subordination of one to the other.

Hegel's later system, as outlined in his *Encyclopedia,* is probably the best example of an attempt to combine dialectic and system in coordinated equipoise. The *Encyclopedia* system is "dialectical" insofar as it is concerned precisely with opposition, *without* the oscillations to and fro that characterize other dialectical philosophical works, such as the classical dialogues just mentioned. The oppositions are brought out as coordinated from the beginning and are presented in tandem; there are no ironical developments such as one finds in Hegel's *Phenomenology,* where the equipoise between dialectic and system is less apparent, and dialectic seems to predominate. For example, in the later system, we do not get immersed in the distinction between being and nothingness and then find, much to our surprise, that being is actually nothingness. Instead, they are shown to be mutually implicated from the very beginning. The Idea, which coordinates subjective and objective aspects, is the ineluctable controlling factor, present at all stages to guarantee that no opposite will be presented in its isolated onesidedness.

VIII. A Historical System

It is a convention now to make a distinction between systematic, problem-oriented philosophy and philosophical study oriented toward the history of philosophy. Anglo-American analytic philosophers are systematic in the sense that they are concerned with solving specific problems related to language or reality, although they do not accept the possibility of a philosophical system. In journals devoted to analytic philosophy, comparatively little attention is given to perspectives on the history of philosophy; the emphasis is on problem solving, and the "conversations" and debates are largely among similarly oriented twentieth-century practitioners. Many analytic philosophers pride themselves on not being "mere historians," but offering fresh and original solutions to new or long-standing problems in metaphysics, epistemology, ethics, and other specialized areas of philosophy.

Historically oriented philosophers, on the other hand, typically focus on historical positions; their conversations and disputes are typically about textual authenticity, appropriate interpretations, and historical influences, and sometimes about possible contemporary applications of some of the more viable, perennial ideas from the past. They pride themselves on being in touch with the intellectual traditions of their civilization, and sometimes warn about the tendency of analytic philosophers to "reinvent the wheel" because of their alleged inattention to what has already been accomplished by their philosophical predecessors.

Hegel belongs to neither of these camps; or rather, he belongs to both. He combines a commitment to solving the major problems of many specialized areas of philosophy with an attention to the history of philosophy greater than that of any other modern philosopher. As was mentioned above, Hegel views the subject-object relationship as *the* perennial problem in western philosophy; and he theorizes that the history of philosophy is really the history of sometimes discordant, sometimes concerted, efforts to arrive at a solution of this problem. Thus in Hegel's view there is in the strict sense only *one* philosophical system, historically evolving as it progresses towards this goal (H1 §8). This viewpoint influenced Hegel's treatment of philosophical problems; in actual practice, Hegel is constantly interweaving approaches to issues or problems with insights about historical antecedents and past progress.

Thus, in his approach, Hegel aims to avoid the twin dangers of "reinventing the wheel" and of becoming a mere historian. But in his ambition to cap off the "one historically evolving system" of philosophy with a final comprehensive approach, does he exceed the limits of what can be done? This is a question that we will need to return to, after developing the multiple facets of his philosophy.

Chapter Two

Phenomenology and System

I. The Current Controversy

There are several "phenomenologies" among Hegel's works. The *Phenomenology of Spirit* (1807), written while Hegel was a professor at the University of Jena, was his first major work, constituting—according to its subtitle—the "First Part" of his "System of Science." In 1808, Hegel took a position as headmaster and instructor at a *Gymnasium* in Nürnberg; while he was there, he wrote a summary (which would be published posthumously) of the first few sections of his Jena *Phenomenology* for these high school students. Pöggeler shows[1] that Hegel had originally intended to cover the whole of the Jena *Phenomenology* in this summary, though he did not accomplish this: the extant summary, the "Propadeutics," covers only about one-third of it. In these years, Hegel still characterized the *Phenomenology* as an integral part of his system. In the Foreword to the "Logic of Being" in the first edition of his *Wissenschaft der Logik* (1813), Hegel speaks of it as the "first part" of his system. In the second edition, however, Hegel announces that the *Phenomenology* will no longer be called the "first part." Later, in the three editions of his *Encyclopedia of Philosophical Sciences,* published when he was a professor—first at Heidelberg and then at Berlin—the shortened form of the *Phenomenology* that he used for instructional purposes in the *Gymnasium* is revised and ostensibly reincorporated into the new *Encyclopedia* version of "Phenomenology," included in the section "Subjective Spirit." In the first edition of the *Encyclopedia* (1817, §36), Hegel emphasizes that presuppositions in philosophy must be eliminated in this encyclopedia, as in the *Phenomenology*. But he also states that the Jena *Phenomenology* was not an "absolute beginning"; and when, in the same paragraph, he goes on to assure his readers that the *Phenomenology* will still "have its place" in the *Encyclopedia,* he appears to be downplaying the importance of the earlier work. In accordance with his objective of incorporating the Jena *Phenomenology,* Part III of the final version of *Encyclopedia* continues to contain the section called "Phenomenology," which retraces the opening chapters of the earlier work, up to the beginning of what was the fifth chapter.

In the opinion of some scholars, Hegel's last two shortened versions of his "phenomenology" have for all practical purposes relativized the status of the Jena *Phenomenology.* Theodore Haering, considering the abbreviated version in the Nürnberg *Propadeutics,* surmised that this indicates some "second thoughts." Haering concludes that in the Jena version, Hegel had intended to stop at the fifth chapter but then got "carried away" and began to fill up the later parts of the book with an assortment of ideas which doubled its intended length, producing a total of eight chapters; later, in writing the "Propadeutics," Hegel recognized his earlier excesses and returned to his original intention (Pöggeler 1973, 199, 205). Michael Petry goes even further in his edition of *The Berlin Phenomenology.* Petry considers the succinct *Encyclopedia* versions of Hegel's phenomenology distinctly superior to earlier versions and concludes that the Jena version was not just relativized but completely replaced by the "Phenomenology" sections of the final two (Berlin) versions of the *Encyclopedia.*[2] Petry is particularly critical of the sections on nature in the Jena version, which in his opinion do not even seem relevant to Hegel's overall intention of examining the modes of consciousness (E2P, 85); but Petry fails to notice that all the sections on nature in the *Phenomenology of Spirit* are more precisely concerned not with nature per se, but with the endeavors of Reason, as a form of consciousness, to find its reflection in nature.[3]

Petry and others who downplay the importance of the Jena *Phenomenology of Spirit* seem to be supported by some of Hegel's own comments on it, penned shortly before his death, while its second edition was being prepared. When he signed the contract for this second edition, Hegel included a note to the effect that the 1807 *Phenomenology of Spirit* was "prefatory to Science," was a "characteristic work from his early years," and was "not to be revised" (PS, 552). He himself, before his untimely death, made only typographical corrections to the Preface of this second edition. But while some have concluded from Hegel's note that the earlier phenomenology is hopelessly outdated, Bonsiepen interprets the note differently: Hegel was not merely relativizing the Jena *Phenomenology* as regards its relationship to the later system but rather was reiterating and clarifying the true significance of the early work.[4]

Just what was the significance of the Jena *Phenomenology* in Hegel's eyes during his professorship at the University of Berlin? Although Hegel did not use it as a text for his lectures, Bonsiepen observes that he made frequent references to various parts of it (Pöggeler 1977, 74). And it should be noted that throughout his *Encyclopedia,* in sections *other than* "Phenomenology," Hegel takes up themes that were initially developed in the Jena *Phenomenology*—for example, the "thing" of perception (E1, §125), Force (E1, §136), organic teleology (E1, §204), Life (E1, §215), the Knight of Virtue (E1, §234, Zusatz), the critique of contemporary theories of irritability and sensibility (E2, §270), the significance of the four elements (E2, §281), language and deeds as the true expression of the mind-body relationship (E3, §411), and Reason (E3, §467, Zusatz). But admittedly, this could be just Hegel's selective reference to, or incorporation of, his earlier ideas. The question about the overall relationship of *Phenomenology of Spirit* to the later system still remains.

Pöggeler maintains that *Phenomenology* remained both an introduction to Hegel's system *and* the first part of it, even after Hegel abandoned the title he initially planned for the *Phenomenology: "System of Philosophy, First Part: Phenomenology of Spirit"* (Pöggeler, 1973, 205). But, he emphasizes, the *Phenomenology* was *not* the only possible introduction to the system. Later, the History of Philosophy seemed to take over that function, at least in the "element of externality" (Pöggeler 1973, 226). Thus *Phenomenology* was an introduction in an immanent sense, insofar as a reading of the *Phenomenology* would pave the way for an understanding of the "absolute" standpoint that was the sine qua non for the development of the system; but the History of Philosophy was also an introduction, insofar as it showed that the succession of philosophies and philosophers up to the present had finally arrived at the standpoint of "absolute knowledge." (Since this succession of philosophies and philosophers is included in highly condensed form in the last chapter of the *Phenomenology* [PSK, §803], one could argue that Hegel is simply using the culminating developments of the *Phenomenology* as his introduction, in lieu of the complete work. If that was the case, it would be more accurate to say that there were not two introductions, because the history of philosophy has *always* served as the primary introduction to the system.)

II. An Aristotelian Analogy

Perhaps the overall relationship of the *Phenomenology* to the later system can best be clarified by returning to the Aristotelian distinction, discussed in Chapter 1, between dialectic and science. Aristotle begins his major works, such as the *Physics, Metaphysics,* and *De Anima,* with a systematic dialectical sifting of opposing positions, in a search for relevant principles and in an attempt to put the issues in their historical context; but then, in the body of these works, Aristotle proceeds to the "scientific" parts, for which dialectic had paved the way. For Aristotle, dialectic was a propaedeutic to science, an approximation to science. Thus, *servatis servandis,* it was also *scientific* insofar as it was oriented to the investigation of first principles and followed the logical rules which Aristotle thought necessary for scientific methodology. But it was not "science proper." And Aristotle, if he were asked about the most significant parts of his system, would certainly have pointed to the scientific elements rather than the dialectical elements. One could conceivably understand the scientific parts of Aristotle's system without reading the dialectical parts and also get a good idea of Aristotle's final positions on the issues discussed—although one would of course miss the contextual-historical context developed in the dialectical sections.

Hegel's Jena *Phenomenology,* like Aristotle's dialectic, was in its author's estimation essentially a propaedeutic to philosophical science, pedagogically necessary to prevent him from defending, like some of his contemporaries, an "Absolute that is shot from guns" (PS, 21), i.e., an Absolute simply presupposed as intuitively evident, and proposed to the scientific community without conscientious groundwork. And in fulfilling this role, Hegel insists, *Phenomenology* is "already Science" (PSK, §88).

III. Is the Berlin "Phenomenology" a Truncated Form of the Jena Version?

When we examine and compare the two phenomenologies, and notice that the later Berlin version includes titles and themes from the first five chapters of the earlier Jena version, it appears offhand that "Phenomenology" in the *Encyclopedia* is indeed just a more concise recapitulation of the first parts of the Jena *Phenomenology of Spirit.* We might go further and conjecture, like Haering, that the later phenomenology is a more accurate version, showing that Hegel had second thoughts about what he should have included in the earlier version. According to this view, the final three chapters of the earlier work were jettisoned as superfluous to the argument; and even themes which were prominent in the first five chapters, such as the lengthy picturesque analysis of the "Unhappy Consciousness" and the passionate search by Reason for the "law of the heart," were completely omitted from the later version.

But if we look more closely, we will find that even though the titles like "Sense Certainty," "Perception," and "Understanding," are the same, the content and treatment of the issues differ markedly. For one thing, there are no ironical developments that seem to come about, so to speak, "behind the back" of consciousness. Consciousness in the attitude of "Sense-certainty" does not enthusiastically extol the truth of particular sense experience, and then find, much to its surprise and chagrin, that truth is really to be found in the universal; Self-Consciousness in its role as Master does not gain its freedom and recognition at the expense of the Slave, and then wake up one day to find that it is actually dependent on the Slave and not really free; Reason does not go out naively searching for evidence of a subjective-objective union in pseudosciences like physiognomy and palmistry and then finally discover, to its dismay, that these sciences do not "deliver" on their promises but only accentuate the mind-body dichotomy. In brief, there are no dialectical oscillations back and forth in the later phenomenology. Consciousness—unlike the interlocutors of Socrates in Plato's dialogues—does not proceed with confidence to a conclusion, only to meet up with contradictions or "dead ends" which mandate revisions and often reversals of its initial certainty.

This ironical type of dialectic is completely lacking in the later system. Hegel, like Aristotle, saw dialectic as a means to an end; and for Hegel the end was Science, or "Speculation." In the *Encyclopedia,* including the section "Phenomenology," dialectical oppositions are once and for all subsumed into the synthesizing Idea. In "Phenomenology" in the *Encyclopedia,* Consciousness does not go through an experience of trying to track down the truth of sense-certainty in "nows" and "heres" but is presented systematically as coordinating spatial and temporal qualities in perceptual "things" and then raising particular things to universality through laws formulated by the Understanding. Self-Consciousness does not go through a trial-and-error process of heroic life-and-death struggles and a master-slave relationship; instead, historical practices such as slavery are presented systematically as imperfect movements toward the final achievement of a universal mutual recognition that can be attained only in the modern state. The oscillations and oppositions which ran rampant in the Jena *Phenomenology* are still present, but *aufgehoben,* superseded in and through the Idea, seen *sub specie aeternitatis.*

Even if one agrees that, a choice being necessary, a systematic-scientific approach in philosophy is *as a general rule* preferable to an oscillating, dialectical approach, it is not completely clear that Hegel's systematic treatment of Consciousness, Self-Consciousness, and Reason in the *Encyclopedia* "Phenomenology" falls under that general rule and is preferable to the treatment of these subjects in the Jena *Phenomenology*. Vittorio Hösle, in his book on Hegel's system,[5] maintains that there are four major deficiencies of the *later* version—"Phenomenology" in the *Encyclopedia*—in comparison with the earlier book, *The Phenomenology of Spirit*. (1) The category "Universal Self-Consciousness" at the end of this subsection should lead directly into the category "Objective Spirit," since there are hardly any other two categories which are so closely intertwined; but instead, a tangential and distracting subsection on "Psychology" separates them. (2) In the Jena *Phenomenology,* the concept of Reason emerged from Self-Consciousness and intersubjectivity, and then led to multiple intersubjective developments throughout the remainder of the book. But in the *Encyclopedia,* since the category of Reason in "Subjective Spirit" has nothing to do with intersubjectivity, and since Hegel in this later system strenuously connects Reason with the ability of Understanding to make "distinctions which are no distinctions," it is hard to understand why Hegel, instead of proceeding directly from Understanding to Reason, goes directly to Self-Consciousness and intersubjectivity, and only thereafter to Reason. The movement to self-consciousness seems like a detour in the context of the *systematic* requirements. (3) The trichotomy of Sense-Certainty, Perception, and Understanding is a purely *linear* succession, since Understanding does not synthesize the previous two stages; one would have expected a *dialectical* succession, in which the third stage superseded but also incorporated the first two stages. (4) In a comprehensive "philosophy of subjective Spirit," one could justifiably expect adequate development of the category of *work*. Hegel analyzes the phenomenology of work in great detail in the Jena *Phenomenology;* but in the *Encyclopedia,* the development of work and the technical (the *poetike* of Aristotle) is relegated to some very brief comments in the section on the Master-Slave relationship—this is a glaring deficiency.

In Hösle's eyes, the most substantial difference in content between the earlier and the later phenomenologies is the minuscule attention given to the problem of intersubjectivity in the later version. According to Hösle, the signal contribution of the Jena *Phenomenology of Spirit* is the dialectical development of the theme of intersubjectivity in multiple applications throughout that work—which anticipates a major area of interest in contemporary philosophy (Hösle 1988, 381-83).

In view of such differences in approach, content, or both, we may conclude that it is at least not obvious that the later phenomenology is just a "revised, updated, clearer" version of the earlier one. But if the earlier phenomenology was not simply superseded by a revised formulation in the later system, what is its role or function?

IV. The Relationship of the Earlier to the Later Phenomenology

As was mentioned above, Hegel initially characterized the *Phenomenology of Spirit* as the "First Part" of his system. This designation becomes ambiguous when we consider the structure of the later tripartite system, in which Logic forms the first part. But in the sense that an introduction can be said to constitute the "first part" of a book—or in the sense that an introductory volume to a tripartite second volume is the "first part" of that opus—the *Phenomenology of Spirit* is still a "First Part." And it is indeed an introduction to Hegel's philosophical system—some might say the best introduction. Possibly this is its most important role.

If a philosopher may be said to have a laboratory, the *Phenomenology of Spirit* was Hegel's laboratory for developing the pivotal notion of an absolute standpoint in philosophy. As was mentioned above, Hegel shared the misgivings of Fichte, Schelling, and others about the problem of the "thing in itself," and about the dualistic epistemology accruing to Kantian critical philosophy. Like them, he wanted to develop an absolute principle that would no longer be infected with such dualism. But, by doing the necessary empirical research beforehand, he wanted to avoid the "absolute shot from guns." Hegel's original title for the Jena *Phenomenology* was "Science of the Experience of Consciousness," though he eventually decided to include this phrase only in his Introduction, to designate the purpose of the work (PSK, §88). The *Phenomenology* is indeed a "science of the experience of consciousness"—a comprehensive and systematic inspection of possible modes in which consciousness may be related to its objects, with a view to arriving finally at an optimal cognitive standpoint where there will no longer be any discrepancy between knowledge and its objects. The various "Moments" and "Configurations" of consciousness in the *Phenomenology* form a "system of consciousness" (PSK, §89), preparing the way for the later presentation of the various categories in the system of the Idea/Spirit. "Absolute Knowledge," with which the *Phenomenology* ends, provides the perspective from which Hegel's *Science of Logic* and other parts of the system are to be understood.

Anyone who approached the later system—say, the *Science of Logic*—without the *Phenomenology* as a background would very likely be mistaken about the context of the analyses: for example, taking the category "Being" (with which Logic begins), in the traditional scholastic objective-ontological sense instead of as a Being-Thought complexus which emerges in Absolute Knowledge. Such a reader would likewise probably miss the religious moorings of the system, i.e., the role of Absolute Knowledge in bringing the imaginative representations of religion to conceptual completeness (PSK, §§802-3); and would be unaware of the "historical credentials" of Absolute Knowledge—the way it has evolved in the history of philosophy (PSK, §§803-4).

Chapter Three
Overview of the System

As has already been indicated, Hegel's system is circular in structure. Both the Jena *Phenomenology of Spirit* as a "system of consciousness" (PS, 68) and the System proper are constructed as philosophical circles. In the following sections, I will discuss how the two works are circular; whether the two circles of the *Phenomenology* and the System are independent or interdependent, asymmetric or parallel; and what the "content" of the respective circles is.

I. The Circularity of the *Phenomenology*

The *Phenomenology* constitutes Hegel's first systematic circle. At the outset of this work, Hegel advises his readers not to expect a concise statement of its goal or purpose and not to expect the goal to be reached by straightforward, linear argumentation. The linear procedure, he says, is normal for other sciences but is not appropriate for philosophy. This can result in some confusion:

> The philosophical proposition, since it *is* a proposition, leads one to believe that the usual subject-predicate relation obtains, as well as the usual attitude towards knowing. But the philosophical content disturbs this attitude and this opinion. . . . Only a philosophical exposition that rigidly excludes the usual way of relating the parts of a proposition could achieve the goal of plasticity. . . . [The dialectical movement of the philosophical Idea] must be expressed; not only must the internal restrictive antithesis be expressed, but the circling back of the Concept upon itself must also be expressed. . . . The *proposition* should tell us the *truth;* . . . the truth is just the dialectical movement, the passage that generates itself, proceeding from and returning to itself (PS, 47–48).

Hegel thus attempts to prepare his readers for the numerous circular movements in the text, movements embodying dialectical oppositions that have been transversed; and for the ultimate movement of "Absolute Knowledge," in which we discover that Spirit, whose phenomenological paths we have been investigating,

24

is in-itself the movement of thought. . . . This movement is the circle returning to itself, a circle which presupposes its beginning and just attains to this beginning at the end (PS, 525).

What does it mean to "attain to the beginning at the end"? Hegel explains: now that this end has finally been reached in Absolute Knowledge,

Science includes within itself the necessity of throwing off the form of the pure Concept [which has just been attained], and the necessity of the transition from the Concept back to Consciousness [i.e., to the initial phenomenological stage]. For self-knowing Spirit, just because it grasps its Concept, is the immediate self-identity that in its [self-]difference is the certitude of immediacy, i.e. Sense-Certainty [Chapter 1],—the beginning from which we set out (PS, 529).

In other words, the immediate self-identity attained in the stage of Absolute Knowledge, because of the ultimate self-differentiation which it also implies, leads Consciousness-Spirit back to its roots—the immediate Sense-Certainty from which all the more sophisticated stages of consciousness, including Absolute Knowledge, began and still begin.

This circling back to the origins of consciousness is, however, just the final outer circle, bringing to a conclusion a number of inner circular movements already transversed. If we omit the many submovements in the *Phenomenology,* the larger picture of the main circular movements of that work can be schematized as shown in Figure 3.

Explanation of Figure 3: (A) The *Phenomenology* begins with Sense-Certainty and other forms of Consciousness in relationship to objectivity, and with attempts to overcome the dualistic disparity or otherness between Consciousness and its objects. Consciousness achieves this goal in the lawmaking operations of "Understanding," in which the objective laws it is dealing with are patently subjective creations. (B) As a result of this experience, it turns to examine the experience of self-consciousness, in which conscious subjectivity becomes its own object. There it finds that it has not escaped otherness. It encounters a new type of otherness in other consciousnesses, and its attempt to disarm this otherness reaches a culmination in a final union with absolute otherness. This union is represented religiously as a union of the human and the divine, but subsequently takes the philosophical form of (C) "Reason," a new un-Kantian faculty which starts with the certainty of the union of consciousness and objectivity, ego and reality. But Reason in its initially abstract stage wants to ascertain the precise locus of this union of self

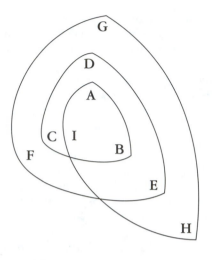

Key

A. Consciousness   D. Observing Reason   G. Spirit
B. Self-Consciousness   E. Self-Conscious Reason   H. Religion
C. Reason   actualizing itself   I. Absolute Knowledge
                           F. Individuality
                              (real in and for itself)

Figure 3. Major structural moments in the *Phenomenology of Spirit*.

and other; thus it begins to search for a subjective-objective union in (D) observation of Nature and in (E) individual self-expression and self-fulfillment. Failing this, it finally finds (F) *die Sache selbst*—the categorial union of ego and otherness—in a special type of individuality, which could be characterized as a "universal individual." But this universal individual presupposes (G) a certain context of social consciousness or "Spirit," and after experiencing much cultural alienation, finds the highest form of Spirit in a Fichtean "church of consciences" and finally in a mutual forgiveness and reconciliation of souls in which the Divine is revealed among humans. (H) The progressive revelation of the Divine in religion is then explored, Christianity being the most concrete form of this revelation. (I) "Absolute Knowledge" finally brings the highly imaginative subjective-objective syntheses of religion to the conceptual level in speculative philosophy. But speculative philosophy *must begin anew* with Sense-Certainty—the point (A) where *Phenomenology* began!

II. The Later System as a Circle of Circles

Hegel is even more explicit about the circularity of the organization of his later system, which begins with the *Science of Logic.* At the end of the *Science of Logic* he offers an initial projection of the type of circular movement that characterizes his system:

> By dint of the demonstrated characteristics of our method, [philosophical] science exhibits itself as a *circle* snaking back upon itself; the process of mediation recoils the end back upon the beginning, the simple ground of the system. The resultant circle is a circle of circles, wherein each individual subdivision, vivified by the method, is a self-reflection that, insofar as it returns back upon its own beginning, is straightway the beginning of a new subdivision. The links of this chain are the individual sciences, each of which has a "before" and an "after," or, more precisely, only *has* the "before," and at its conclusion just *points out* its "after" (SL2, 572).

But Logic is not the only part of the system that is methodologically circular. Hegel notes in the first edition of the *Encyclopedia* that the total System—consisting of Logic, Philosophy of Nature and Philosophy of Spirit—is a circle of circles:

> Insofar as philosophy is a thoroughly rational Science, each of its parts is a philosophical whole, a self-enclosing circle of totality; but the philosophical Idea is present there in a special determinacy or element. Each particular circle, since it is in-itself the totality, thus also breaks through the limitations of its element and supplies the grounding for a wider sphere. Hence the whole presents itself as a circle of circles, each of these circles being a necessary moment. The result is that the System of the special elements expresses the entire Idea; and the Idea likewise shines forth in each of its elements (E1, §5).

Hegel emphasizes the circularity of the System in somewhat more precise language toward the end of the *Encyclopedia* as a "system-syllogism" in which each of the three component elements functions in turn as the syllogistic "major," "minor," or "conclusion" for the others (E1, §§475–77). This metaphorical emphasis on the methodological circularity of the system is continued in the later editions of the *Encyclopedia of Philosophical Sciences* (E1, §§15, 17; E3, §575–77).

The circular interrelationship of the various parts of the *Encyclopedia* system as a whole can be schematized as shown in Figure 4 (again, leaving out many subordinate movements).

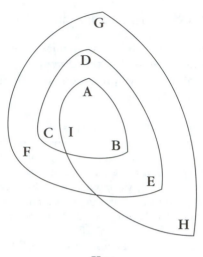

Key

A. Being	D. Mechanics	G. Objective Spirit
B. Essence	E. Physics	H. Subjective Spirit
C. Concept	F. Organics	I. Absolute Spirit

Figure 4. Major structural moments in the *Encyclopedia.*

Explanation of Figure 4: (A) The indeterminate "Being" that we start out with reveals itself as harboring qualitative and quantitative determinations, and finally the category of "Measure," which involves a paradoxical convergence of quantity and quality. This convergence of opposites leads to (B) "Essence," which is characterized by polarities or oppositions that no longer need to be demonstrated or deduced but are immediately patent and explicit. Included among such polarities are essence-existence, substance-accident, inner-outer, reality-appearance, and cause-effect. Eventually, the emergence of the paradoxical notion of a "reciprocal" causality, where cause and effect converge, leads to the development of (C) the "Concept." This is not the abstract concept of the understanding, but a concrete Concept characterized by dynamic unities-in-distinction. These unities-in-distinction are exemplified *subjectively* by the syllogism, which captures the rationality of reality; *objectively* by teleology, which unifies particularity and universality; and *absolutely* in the rational-reality or particularized universality of Life, Cognition, and Willing (the absolute Idea).

But the absolute Idea possesses *otherness* in itself and produces itself as otherness in Nature—which, being outside the Idea, is characterized by considerable chance and contingencies. Still, Nature approximates the Idea in three stages: (D) universality of space, time, and matter; (E) particularity of physical phenomena like gravity, sound, heat, magnetism, electricity, and chemical reactions; and (F) individuality (i.e., universalized particularity) of living organisms, which ultimately raise the manifolds of physics to subjective unity.

As life emerges in nature, the Idea becomes explicit, first (G) as Subjective Spirit passing from unconsciousness to the "Phenomenology" of consciousness and self-consciousness, and to the higher stages of cognition and will; then (H) as Objective Spirit embodied in familial and political organizations and corollary systems of rights and laws; and finally [I] as Absolute Spirit, in which Spirit rises to ultimate self-consciousness in art, religion, and philosophy. And since philosophy is primarily concerned with *Being,* this ultimate stage of Spirit is in effect a *return* to the Idea in its abstract form in the Logic, the beginning of the *Encyclopedia*!

III. Interrelationships and Correspondences

Even among scholars who agree that the Jena *Phenomenology of Spirit* is important in its own right, and not superseded by the later phenomenologies, there is disagreement as to whether the two systems—the *Phenomenology* as a system of consciousness, and the *Encyclopedia* as the System proper—are structurally related to each other.

Otto Pöggeler maintains that the Jena *Phenomenology* corresponds clearly only to a projection Hegel made of his future system *prior to* the publication of the *Phenomenology* (Pöggeler 1973, 222, 226). Hegel, in his *Realphilosophie* of 1805–1806, had formulated the idea of a system of philosophy consisting of six parts—(1) Being, (2) Relation, (3) Life and Cognition, (4) Knowing Knowledge, (5) Spirit, and (6) Self-Knowledge of Spirit. The *Phenomenology,* written after the *Realphilosophie,* was, according to Pöggeler, patterned in six corresponding parts, as shown in Figure 5.

Thus, in Pöggeler's interpretation, the first chapter of the *Phenomenology,* "Sense-Certainty," was meant to show the approach to Being from the point of view of Consciousness; "Perception" and "Understanding" (the second and third chapters) were meant to lead into a categorial analysis of Relation; "The Truth of Self-Certainty" (the fourth chapter) would introduce the category-genus of Life; and so forth. But Pöggeler finds no discernible correspondence between the 1807 *Phenomenology* and the *later* system.

Categories in 1805–1806 System	Phenomenological Stages, 1807
Being	Sense-Certainty
Relation	Perception and Understanding
Life	Truth of Self-Certainty
Knowing Knowledge	Reason
Spirit	Spirit
Self-Knowledge of Spirit	Religion and Absolute Knowledge

Figure 5. Correspondences between the *Realphilosophie* (1805–1806) and the *Phenomenology* (1807).

Hegel does indicate, however, toward the end of the *Phenomenology,* that there *will* be a correspondence between the configurations treated there and the categories of his later system:

In general, to each of the abstract Moments of [philosophical] Science there corresponds a configuration of appearing [phenomenological] Spirit. Just as Spirit in its existence is not richer than Science, so also Spirit in its content is not poorer than Science. When the pure concepts [categories] of Science are known in their present form (as configurations of consciousness), this brings out the aspect of their reality; after this, their essence, the Concept, which is established in them as thought in simple mediation, breaks the Moments of this mediation apart and is exhibited [in philosophical Science] according to its inner opposition (PS, 529).

The promise this holds forth for the reader is that in a later scientific system, various dialectical moments of opposition which have appeared in the course of the *Phenomenology of Spirit* will be presented again, in the form of simple categorial mediations of thought. Possibly no one-to-one correspondence is indicated; but some correspondence would be expected. Did Hegel simply abandon this objective when he developed his later system?

Denise Souche-Dagues maintains that we should take Hegel at his word—that the Jena *Phenomenology* is his system of philosophy "as reflected in consciousness," and that he had this in mind in developing his system of categories.[1] And Robert Grant McRae goes even further in trying to work out the phenomenological and categorial correspondences.[2] In assessing McRae's thesis, we have to keep in mind that Hegel revised the organization of his System in certain respects between 1813 and 1831 (this reorganization will be discussed in Chapter 4), so it is necessary to concentrate just on the larger segments and to use generic terminology. But if we adhere to these restrictions and build on McRae's suggestions, with some adaptations, the correspondences between the *Phenomenology* and the later System will look something like Figure 6.

Major sections of *Phenomenology of Spirit*	Correspondences with Hegel's later system
Sense-Certainty and Perception	Objective Logic (science of Being and Essence)
Understanding	Subjective Logic (science of Concept)
Truth of Self-Certainty	Subjective Concept
Reason	Idea
Observing Reason	Philosophy of Nature
Self-Actualizing Reason	Subjective Spirit
Spirit	Objective Spirit: Family, Civil Society, and State
Religion	Absolute Spirit: Art and Religion
Absolute Knowledge	Absolute Spirit: Philosophy

Figure 6. Correspondences between *Phenomenology* and Hegel's later system.

Following the rationale of these correlations, Sense-Certainty would orient Consciousness to the category of Being, and Perception would orient it to the category of Relation. Understanding would prepare the way for the category of Concept; Reason would introduce the Idea (the special technical meanings of "Reason" and "Idea" in Hegel will be discussed in Chapter 4); Observing Reason (concerned in the *Phenomenology* with inorganic and organic nature and the human psyche) would lead to the Philosophy of Nature; Self-Actualizing Reason (*Die Verwirklichung des vernünftigen Selbstbewußtseins durch sich selbst*) would lead to Subjective Spirit; the stages of Spirit in the *Phenomenology* (ethicality, law, culture, Enlightenment, absolute liberty) would correspond to Objective Spirit in the later system; Religion would correspond to the subsections on Art and Religion in the section on Absolute Spirit; and Absolute Knowledge would correspond to the final subsection—Philosophy—in the section on Absolute Spirit.

IV. The Branching Out of the Later System

Almost all of Hegel's teaching and writing, including his posthumously published lectures, expands on the various parts of the outline (*Grundriß*) presented in his *Enzyklopädie der philosophischen Wissenschaften im Grundrisse*. Leaving out fragments and articles, the flowchart in Figure 7 brings out the major interconnections.

Figure 7 helps to highlight two important considerations about Hegel's system as a whole. First, the compendious two-volume *Science of Logic* (1813–1816), which goes into much more detail than the Logic in any of the editions (1817, 1827, 1830) of the *Encyclopedia,* is nevertheless in some respects *structurally* superseded by the later, so-called "lesser" Logic. For in some places the organization of categories, the context of analysis, or both are changed in the later work—in many cases, indicating revisions or more mature treatments of the subject matter. Some of these changes will be discussed in Chapter 4.

Second, the massive multivolume lectures from the Berlin period are all on the final segments of the *Encyclopedia* system. One would justifiably surmise that Hegel's mature interests gravitated away from Logic and Philosophy of Nature to political philosophy; to the philosophies of history, art, and religion; and to the history of philosophy (this last being, for Hegel, a metaphilosophy). The fact that Hegel devoted most of his mature efforts to these subjects does not necessarily mean that he is at his best in these areas. But most Hegel scholarship is still devoted

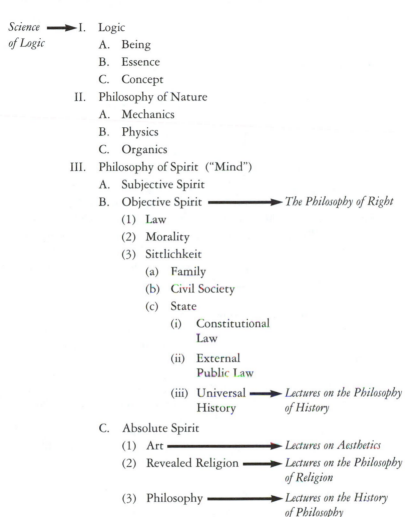

Science ➝ I. Logic
of Logic   A. Being
            B. Essence
            C. Concept
     II. Philosophy of Nature
            A. Mechanics
            B. Physics
            C. Organics
     III. Philosophy of Spirit ("Mind")
            A. Subjective Spirit
            B. Objective Spirit ➝ *The Philosophy of Right*
               (1) Law
               (2) Morality
               (3) Sittlichkeit
                   (a) Family
                   (b) Civil Society
                   (c) State
                       (i) Constitutional Law
                       (ii) External Public Law
                       (iii) Universal ➝ *Lectures on the Philosophy* History *of History*
            C. Absolute Spirit
               (1) Art ➝ *Lectures on Aesthetics*
               (2) Revealed Religion ➝ *Lectures on the Philosophy of Religion*
               (3) Philosophy ➝ *Lectures on the History of Philosophy*

Figure 7. Divisions of the *Encyclopedia of Philosophical Sciences*, third edition.

to Hegel's earlier interests—the *Phenomenology* and the Logic. Possibly the ongoing development of critical editions and translations of the lectures will help to remedy this imbalance.

Chapter Four

Methodological and Stylistic Considerations

I. Hegelian Terminology

One of Hegel's objectives was to "make philosophy speak German." In his *Science of Logic,* he prides himself on the fact that the German language is able to bring out the full speculative meaning of terms like *aufheben* (SL1, 114). Although he has serious criticisms of the philosophy of Christian Wolff in his *Lectures on the History of Philosophy,* he congratulates Wolff on writing his works in German:

> Wolff wrote in German. Tschirnhausen and Thomasius also get credit for this. Leibniz, in contrast, wrote only in Latin or French. But . . . it is only when a science is possessed in the mother tongue that one can say it really belongs to the people. In philosophy in particular, this aspect of "belonging" is of the utmost importance. For thought entails the "moment" in which it belongs to self-consciousness, i.e. becomes its own most "owned" possession. When concepts are expressed in our own language, e.g. *"Bestimmtheit"* instead of "determination," *"Wesen"* instead of [the Latinized] *"Essenz,"* etc., then the fact that the concepts are really "owned," and that it has only to deal with them and not with something foreign, is obvious to consciousness (HP3, 258-59).

Hegel's dedication to Germanicizing philosophy sometimes led him to wordplay: for example, between *meinen* ("to have an opinion") and *meinem* (dative case of the possessive adjective "mine" [PSK, §100]) and between *eigener Sinn* ("a mind of one's own") and *Eigensinn* ("stubbornness" [PSK, §196]). It also sometimes led him to use words in their etymological sense: for example, *Erinnerung* ("recollection") in the sense of *Er-Innerung,* ("making inner" or "assimilation"); *abstrakt* and *Konkret* in the sense of the Latin, *abstrahere* and *concresco; Logik* in the sense of the Greek λόγος and so forth. This causes difficulties for translators—especially when the German terms that Hegel uses are his own translations from other languages.

The Greek Hegel scholar Georgia Apostolopoulou brings this out with regard to the special problems contemporary Greek translators of Hegel face in retranslating into modern Greek terms that Hegel originally translated from ancient Greek into German:

> The Hegelian text is so complicated in its sentence-structure and terminology, that it frequently leads the translator into embarrassment, or more precisely, into a situation of hermeneutical conflict. One might think that the translation [by Hegel] of the Greek terms that are presented to us in Hegel's *Lectures on the History of Philosophy* would be helpful in this regard. But this is not the case, since Hegel at one and the same time is interpreting and translating in the light of his own philosophy, without striving unconditionally for terminological univocity. Thus he translates the word, *"νοῦς"* as *"Intelligenz,"* as *"Verstand,"* or even as *"Gedanke,"* but he sometimes also translates *"λόγος"* as *"Verstand."* Moreover, in the language of modern Greece, for each of the terms that Hegel uses for a rendition of *"νοῦς,"* there is a different corresponding term; thus, for example, *"Intelligenz"* would be translated as *"νοημοσύνη,"* *"Verstand"* as *"διάνοια,"* or *"Gedanke"* as *"σκέψη."* Still another difficulty emerges with reference to the term, *"οὐσία,"* which Hegel sometimes translates as *"Wesen"* and sometimes as *"Substanz"*—while he also at times translates the term *"ὑπόστασῃ"* as *"Substanz."* Correspondingly, in the language of modern Greek philosophy, the term, *"οὐσία,"* is used as a rendition of the term, *"Wesen,"* while the Hegelian term, *"Substanz,'"* is rendered as *"ὑπόστασῃ."*[1]

In view of the tendency of certain continental philosophers to create neologisms, there is an ongoing debate: should philosophy have a special technical terminology, or should it use ordinary language for the most part, as Plato did? As was mentioned above, Hegel often uses terms in an etymological sense; he also sometimes uses adjectives, adverbs, or prepositional phrases in unwonted ways—e.g. "the This" (PSK, §95), "the Here" (PSK, §92), "the Now" (PSK, §92), "the Beyond" (PSK, §212), "the This-side" (PSK, §221), "the in-itself" (PSK, passim), "the Unconscious" (PSK, §472). But such innovations remain close to the meaning of the words from which they are derived. What one must be particularly careful about in Hegel's philosophy is his tendency to use *ordinary* words in a special, technical sense—as Heidegger does with *"Dasein"* and Sartre does with *"le Neant."* Misunderstanding such terms causes confusion in reading Hegel; understanding them is a key to clarifying his ideas. The three primary, pivotal technical terms whose meaning must be understood before any appreciation of Hegel's system is possible are the Idea, the Concept, and Reason.

The *Idea* is to be distinguished from all ordinary, finite abstract "ideas." Hegel uses this term in much the same sense that Kant talks about the "ideas" of God, freedom, and immortality in his *Critique of Pure Reason*. But whereas Kant portrays these ideas disparagingly, as metaphysical constructs which proceed beyond the limits of experience to rather hypothetical (purely "regulative") totalizations, Hegel presents the Idea (embodied in these Kantian "ideas" and also in other instantiations) as the pinnacle of thought, the point at which thought possesses itself once and for all, and becomes "self-thinking thought." Kant himself, Hegel maintains, went beyond the pejorative connotations of the "idea" in his *Critique of Pure Reason,* and arrived in his *Critique of Judgment* at the threshold of the true, speculative Idea—although he did not seem to appreciate his own discovery. For in the technical sense, the Hegelian Idea is just a speculative expansion of a tentative suggestion by Kant[2] of the conceivability of a nondiscursive, nonpassive, spontaneous type of "intellectual intuition," which would not be subject to divisions between particular and universal, subjective and objective, etc. Hegel saw this as a major insight, but he carried it beyond its purely hypothetical parameters in his early essay on *Faith and Knowledge,*[3] and finally presented the Idea in his *Encyclopedia* system as an Absolute encompassing all major oppositions and polarities:

> The Idea can be comprehended as Reason, as the Subject-Object, as the unity of the ideal and the real, the finite and the infinite, the soul and the body; as the possibility that holds its actuality in itself, and thus as that whose "nature" can only be grasped as "existing." . . . The Idea . . . is . . . itself the dialectic which eternally keeps the self-identical apart from the different, the subjective from the objective, . . . the finite from the infinite, the soul from the body, and precisely because of this dialectic is eternal creativity, eternal vitality, and eternal Spirit (H1, §162).

Hegel's Idea is in certain respects comparable to Plato's idea (εἶδος) of the Good, which Plato in some places[4] portrays as not only hierarchically preeminent, but also generative of all subordinate ideas. The Idea has a comparable preeminence for Hegel; there are indeed many ideas, but only one Idea. The Idea is a unique category with multiple instantiations or expressions.

So, also, there are many concepts, but only one Concept. The *Concept* (*Begriff*) is a preliminary, subjective form of the Idea; as the etymological connection of *Begriff* with *greifen* ("to grasp") indicates, it logically and scientifically "grasps together"—comprehends—the various oppositions. It reaches beyond its subjective compass into the otherness of objectivity, until it finally attains to the dialectical equipoise of the Idea. Thus the Concept in all its forms grasps the unity of subject and object, but from a still subjective vantage point (E1, §160, Zusatz; §§164, 193, 214); the Idea, on the other hand, has surpassed the modality of subjectivity and thus is "absolute" in the strict sense.

Reason is another important technical term in Hegel's system. It functions as a kind of faculty for apprehending the Idea; but it is not just a faculty of consciousness. It is more precisely the Idea itself, actualizing itself and becoming conscious of itself. It is not unrelated to Schelling's definition of Reason as "the total indifference of the subjective and the objective," i. e., a standpoint which does not veer either into subjectivity or objectivity.[5] It does what reason could not do in Kant's *Critique of Pure Reason*—it goes beyond the antitheses generated by the Understanding to produce synthetic totalities not conditioned by first-order sense experience.[6] Reason produces its "unities in opposition" in a preliminary way in nature; then more effectively in human relations, history, and the state; and in an ultimate way in art, religion and philosophy.

Hegel's system is not "rationalistic" or "idealistic" in a subjectivistic sense, but it emphasizes the rationality of reality and finds pursuits that we might call "aesthetic," "spiritual," "intellectual," or "rational" to be the ultimate *realities*.

II. "Necessity" in Hegel's System

In his Logic, and elsewhere, Hegel treats the category of necessity in its relationship to possibility, actuality, contingency, and freedom (e.g., SL2, 200ff.). But when he refers to a "necessity" which accrues to the development of this or that category in his philosophical system, what he has in mind is not this categorial necessity but a necessity that comes from the system itself:

> The Science of the Idea is necessarily a *System,* since truth as *concrete* exists only as self-enfolding and coordinating and uniting, i.e., as a *totality;* and the truth can be the necessity of the distinctions and the freedom of the whole only through their differentiation and determination.
>
> Philosophizing *without a System* cannot be scientific; aside from the fact that this sort of philosophizing of itself expresses merely subjective impressions, the philosophy is contingent as regards content (E1, §14).

In the Preface to the *Phenomenology* (the Preface was written after the *Phenomenology* itself and introduces the forthcoming philosophical system), Hegel uses an organic metaphor to clarify the necessary interrelationship between philosophical systems. It seems that one philosophical system is eventually refuted by another, but like the bud that disappears when the blossom appears, or the blossom that disappears when the fruit comes, the philosophical systems which "die out" are necessary developments, without which the one ongoing system of philosophy could not progress (PS, 4). The same organic metaphor could be applied to the various categories of Hegel's later System, which supersede one another under the teleological impetus of the Idea. Being seems to fall by the wayside as Existence and Quality come to the fore; the distinction between Quality and Quantity seems to disappear as the category of Measure/Degree becomes prominent; and so forth. These are all "necessary" moments, Hegel maintains.

But what, then, are we to say of the changes and revisions which Hegel himself made in the organization of the categories in successive elaborations of his system from 1813 to 1831? Some categories seem to have disappeared, or to have been repositioned in another part of the system. Would this imply that the categories in question are not so unequivocally necessary? Or does it perhaps imply that only the final version of the categories—in the third edition of the *Encyclopedia*—really captures the systematic categorial necessity? The revisions are in a few cases quite substantial, as Figures 8 and 9 show.

In Figures 8 and 9, some of the differences in titles do not indicate substantial changes in categorial organization. For example, the subcategories under "Measure" in the *Science of Logic* merely indicate that the treatment of Measure is much more detailed in this work than in the *Encyclopedia* (the treatment in the *Science of Logic* is in fact ten times as long). And sometimes a title which seems different in one version is actually used synonymously with titles in other versions. For example, the subcategory "The Absolute Relation" within the category "Reality" in the *Science of Logic* is synonymous in Hegel's *Encyclopedia* system with the relation of Reciprocity; thus "Reciprocity" is designated as the subcategory in subsequent versions.

But there also seem to be some substantial revisions. Hösle, for instance, notes that the extremely wide-ranging revisions between the Heidelberg and Berlin periods in Hegel's second section of Philosophy of Nature (Physics) indicates that Hegel encountered numerous problems in his development of this section (Hösle 1988, 287n). The discrepancy between "Mathematics" and "Mechanics" as the starting point for a philosophy of Nature is just the beginning of many other discrepancies:

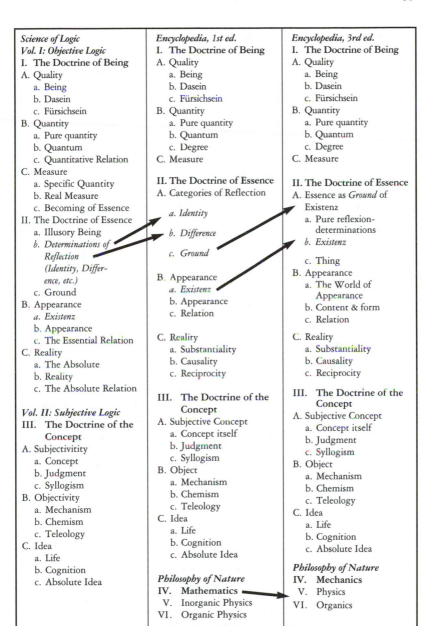

Science of Logic
Vol. I: Objective Logic
I. The Doctrine of Being
A. Quality
   a. Being
   b. Dasein
   c. Fürsichsein
B. Quantity
   a. Pure quantity
   b. Quantum
   c. Quantitative Relation
C. Measure
   a. Specific Quantity
   b. Real Measure
   c. Becoming of Essence
II. The Doctrine of Essence
   a. Illusory Being
   b. *Determinations of Reflection* (Identity, Difference, etc.)
   c. Ground
B. Appearance
   a. *Existenz*
   b. Appearance
   c. The Essential Relation
C. Reality
   a. The Absolute
   b. Reality
   c. The Absolute Relation

Vol. II: Subjective Logic
III. The Doctrine of the Concept
A. Subjectivity
   a. Concept
   b. Judgment
   c. Syllogism
B. Objectivity
   a. Mechanism
   b. Chemism
   c. Teleology
C. Idea
   a. Life
   b. Cognition
   c. Absolute Idea

Encyclopedia, 1st ed.
I. The Doctrine of Being
A. Quality
   a. Being
   b. Dasein
   c. Fürsichsein
B. Quantity
   a. Pure quantity
   b. Quantum
   c. Degree
C. Measure

II. The Doctrine of Essence
A. Categories of Reflection
   a. *Identity*
   b. *Difference*
   c. *Ground*
B. Appearance
   a. *Existenz*
   b. Appearance
   c. Relation
C. Reality
   a. Substantiality
   b. Causality
   c. Reciprocity

III. The Doctrine of the Concept
A. Subjective Concept
   a. Concept itself
   b. Judgment
   c. Syllogism
B. Object
   a. Mechanism
   b. Chemism
   c. Teleology
C. Idea
   a. Life
   b. Cognition
   c. Absolute Idea

Philosophy of Nature
IV. Mathematics
V.   Inorganic Physics
VI. Organic Physics

Encyclopedia, 3rd ed.
I. The Doctrine of Being
A. Quality
   a. Being
   b. Dasein
   c. Fürsichsein
B. Quantity
   a. Pure quantity
   b. Quantum
   c. Degree
C. Measure

II. The Doctrine of Essence
A. Essence as *Ground* of Existenz
   a. Pure reflexion-determinations
   b. *Existenz*
   c. Thing
B. Appearance
   a. The World of Appearance
   b. Content & form
   c. Relation
C. Reality
   a. Substantiality
   b. Causality
   c. Reciprocity

III. The Doctrine of the Concept
A. Subjective Concept
   a. Concept itself
   b. Judgment
   c. Syllogism
B. Object
   a. Mechanism
   b. Chemism
   c. Teleology
C. Idea
   a. Life
   b. Cognition
   c. Absolute Idea

Philosophy of Nature
IV. Mechanics
V.   Physics
VI. Organics

Figure 8. Comparison of versions of Hegel's system: *Science of Logic* and first and third editions of the *Encyclopedia*, up to *Philosophy of Spirit*.

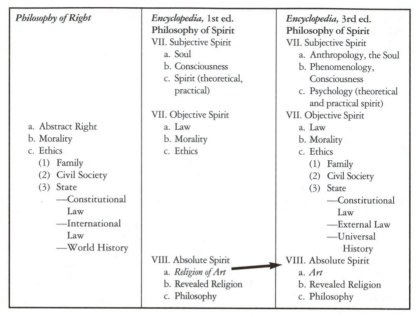

Philosophy of Right	Encyclopedia, 1st ed. Philosophy of Spirit	Encyclopedia, 3rd ed. Philosophy of Spirit
	VII. Subjective Spirit	VII. Subjective Spirit
	a. Soul	a. Anthropology, the Soul
	b. Consciousness	b. Phenomenology, Consciousness
	c. Spirit (theoretical, practical)	c. Psychology (theoretical and practical spirit)
	VII. Objective Spirit	VII. Objective Spirit
a. Abstract Right	a. Law	a. Law
b. Morality	b. Morality	b. Morality
c. Ethics	c. Ethics	c. Ethics
(1) Family		(1) Family
(2) Civil Society		(2) Civil Society
(3) State		(3) State
—Constitutional Law		—Constitutional Law
—International Law		—External Law
—World History		—Universal History
	VIII. Absolute Spirit	VIII. Absolute Spirit
	a. Religion of Art	a. Art
	b. Revealed Religion	b. Revealed Religion
	c. Philosophy	c. Philosophy

Figure 9. Comparison of versions of Hegel's system: *Encyclopedia* and *Philosophy of Right*.

The "Mathematics" of the Heidelberg Encyclopedia coincides only with the first section of the later [Berlin] "Mechanics," which treated of space, time and motion; on the other hand, the two other [Berlin] sections—on finite and absolute mechanics—constitute in the Heidelberg Encyclopedia the first section of the second division, "inorganic physics." In this earlier [Heidelberg] segmentation real physical matter is considered in the second part of the Philosophy of Nature; the first part comprises only "universal, ideal otherness-to-self." Of course, it can't be said that this [Heidelberg] division is the original one for Hegel. Indeed this ordering is found also in the encyclopedia of the *Propadeutic* for the upper classes [of the *Gymnasium*], where "natural science" comprises "mathematics," "physics," and "organic physics," and Mechanics belongs to the second part. But the Philosophy of Nature of the [even earlier] Jena System-projections either supposes a twofold division into the sun-and earth-system (*Systemwürfe* I), or, better, develops this division explicitly (*Systemwürfe* II), or has a threefold division comparable to that of the Berlin Encyclopedia (*Systemwurf* III) (Hösle 1988, 289-90).

The changes in organization seem substantial in a philosophy of nature which claims systematic necessity. We see that such subjects as finite and absolute mechanics, and real physical matter, are considered in the second subdivision of the Heidelberg *Encyclopedia* but are transferred thirteen years later to the first subdivision of the Berlin *Encyclopedia;* and that the Heidelberg subdivisions of 1817 parallel the subdivisions made for the *Gymnasium* in Nürnberg, But the subdivisions of the *Encyclopedia* in 1830 parallel the subdivisions of *Systemwürfe III* (1805-1806). As we examine these changes, we get an impression not of the Concept of Nature developing itself as a necessity, but of a philosopher struggling to keep up with the physical sciences, and hoping to be able to give direction to them through the "pure Concept" of Nature, which is supposed to be impervious to the changes taking place in the special sciences.

Hegel's interpretation of the Philosophy of Nature as partly dependent on the empirical sciences, and partly giving direction to the sciences, will be discussed in Chapter 6. If a Philosophy of Nature is indeed conditioned by current scientific theories, one would expect it to reflect changes in the empirical arena. Hösle observes that Hegel was extraordinarily well- versed in the science of his day; but unfortunately that science was often mistaken. The numerous changes in organization of topics in Hegel's Philosophy of Nature were due partially to the inchoate state of science on many of the issues he wanted to discuss in this section of the *Encyclopedia*.

Hösle also finds considerable discrepancy in the organization of the parts of the *Science of Logic* and the presumably corresponding parts of the Logic in the *Encyclopedia*. The first thing one notices is that *Science of Logic* is basically bipartite, objective and subjective, a bifurcation to which the tripartite divisions—Being, Essence, Concept—are subordinate; the Logic, in all versions of the *Encyclopedia,* is tripartite. This discrepancy in form may be taken as a sign of Hegel's constant attempt to overcome dualism, although with regard to content he ends up partially reinstating "Subjective Logic" from the *Science of Logic* in the "Doctrine of the Concept" in the *Encyclopedia,* where one would expect the subjective-objective dichotomy to be overcome:

> Considered *formally,* the tripartite division of the [later] Logic indeed presents a definite advance over against the [earlier] dichotomy into objective and subjective logic; but as regards *content* only this dualistic division of the subject-matter fits; in other words, what is treated in the [later] Logic of the Concept, at least in the first section of this logic, actually belongs not in a concluding [third] part, but in a second part, of the logic as a whole . . . (Hösle, 117).

Hösle's criticism of Hegel's categorial organization has to do with an important prima facie inconsistency: Hegel obviously wants to proceed dialectically, so that the third member of the various triads will truly supersede the subjective-objective oppositions; but he seems to end up here with a linear, not truly speculative, development—a return to subjectivity. The formal change to a tripartite division indicates that he wants to avoid this; but to be successful as regards *content,* he would have to include clearly subjective subject matter in the second division of the later Logic, the Doctrine of Essence, which he characterizes as the "Concept for-itself." Hösle believes that Hegel was much more successful in accomplishing his intentions in the Philosophy of Spirit, where the clearly subjective categories appear in the second segment of the triads in which they belong. For example, in the subtriad of the philosophy of Subjective Spirit, the Ego—the antithesis to the object—appears in the second part, "Phenomenology"; in the subtriad of the philosophy of Objective Spirit, the most subjective stage, Morality, constitutes the second part; in Absolute Spirit, lyric poetry and the subjective relation to God are placed in the second parts of their respective sub-subtriads (Hösle, 218).

Hösle's observation may help to explain the significant changes in the placement of the categories Identity, Difference, Existenz, and Ground in the earlier and later versions of Doctrine of Essence in Logic. Possibly Hegel was becoming more and more conscious of a need for proper dialectic placement of the moments of subjectivity and antithesis. The most noteworthy change in placement between the earlier and later versions is the shift of the category Existenz from the earlier antithetical (second) stage of Doctrine of Essence to the (first) thesis stage in the later version, presumably to emphasize the immediacy of Existence and the parallelism with the position of Dasein in Doctrine of Being. Similarly, the determinations of Identity, Difference, and Ground may have been deemed more "immediate" than "Illusory Being" for Hegel's purposes in the later work.

As Hösle notes, the latter sections of Hegel's system seem to be more consistent with his dialectical-speculative intentions; correspondingly, there seem to be fewer changes in these sections. One significant change, however, may be the shift in categorization from "Religion of Art" in the first edition of the *Encyclopedia* (which is reminiscent of the configuration Art-Religion in the *Phenomenology of Spirit*) to simply "Art" in the third edition, where art as an intuitive approach and religion as an imaginative approach to the Absolute become two separate, independent stepping-stones to Philosophy as the final conceptual approach.

To repeat our earlier question: in view of the sometimes considerable alterations in the position of categories, just what are we to make of the alleged "necessity" of these categories? If a category has the quality of necessity in the *Science of Logic,* how can it be moved to quite another position in the Logic in the last edition of the *Encyclopedia?* One answer is that the question may arise from our tendency to understand "necessity" in the categorial sense discussed above, whereas "necessity," as applied to the system and its parts (even to the category of necessity as a part of the system), seems to have a different and less rigid connotation than "necessity" as a logical category. Another answer—if we want to maintain that Hegel did see the categories as "necessary" in the strict logical sense—is that we simply have to conclude that the third edition of the *Encyclopedia* is Hegel's last word on this, his final interpretation of the necessary interrelationship of the categories of the Logic and the categories of the *Realphilosophie* of Nature and Spirit.

III. Hegel's Use of Metaphors and Similes

Metaphorical language has a long and somewhat honorable tradition in western philosophy. The ancient Greeks described the soul (ψῡχή) as "breath"; Socrates described his philosophical role as that of midwife; Plato described human life as a cave and love as a child. Aristotle tried to avoid metaphors—and similes—in strict philosophical argument, but nevertheless he referred to the active intellect as a "state of light"; he compared a living creature to a well-governed city, with the heart as the center of authority; and he used sculpture as a metaphor for matter-form. Medieval scholastics applied Aristotle's metaphor of sculpture to the divine and supernatural and could not resist bringing out the etymological connection between "matter" and "mother" (*mater*). In modern philosophy—despite Francis Bacon's criticism of metaphors as "idols" of philosophy—metaphor still prevails. Kant made conspicuous efforts to avoid figurative language, but he still needed to refer to the mind as an "instrument" (K-CPR, A61=B86) and described the "cosmological proof" of the existence of God as a "nest of contradictions" (K-CPR, B637). In twentieth-century philosophy, some of the most influential ideas have been metaphorical: William James's "stream of consciousness," Wittgenstein's "family resemblances," Ryle's "ghost in the machine," Derrida's "deconstruction."

One constant amid all the variables in the history of philosophy has been a striving for more accurate modes of expression, even when it is admitted that an expression cannot be exact. But many of the terms philosophers use are at least etymologically metaphorical. Anyone with some knowledge of Latin or Greek cannot help connecting "form" with statuary, "concept" with biological conception, "substance" with location beneath some superstructure, "abstract" with a process of separation, "dialectic" with picking and choosing, "hypothesis" with a foundation, "matter" with a species of abstract maternity. Possibly the best strategy for philosophers is to simply recognize the metaphorical and analogical associations of even the most abstract terms.

Hegel made no effort to avoid metaphorical language in his argumentation, and some of his philosophical explanations are replete with metaphors and similes. Several differences between the Jena *Phenomenology of Spirit* and "Phenomenology" in the *Encyclopedia* have been discussed in detail above; but an additional difference is the frequent use of metaphor in the earlier phenomenology. In the chapter on Sense-Certainty in the *Phenomenology,* sensation is likened to participation in the ancient Eleusinian mysteries of Ceres and Bacchus (PSK, §109); in discussing the close relationship between brain and mind, Hegel compares it to Nature's joke of combining lowly urination and sublime procreation in the same bodily organ (PS, 233); and in criticizing Kant's theory of morality, Hegel turns Kant's own metaphor—"nest of contradictions"— against him (PSK, §617). Also, in *Phenomenology,* after the stage of Self-Consciousness has been attained, a series of metaphorical tableaus are developed in tandem with the advances to more sophisticated stages of consciousness: Master versus Slave and a monkish "unhappy consciousness" in the fourth chapter; a "Knight of Virtue" in the fifth chapter; the "Noble and Base" consciousnesses, the "Distraught" consciousness, the "Beautiful Soul," and the "Acting Consciousness" in the sixth chapter; and so forth. Hegel uses such metaphors to unify and define the more and more complex stages that emerge in his "system of consciousness."

In the *Science of Logic,* Hegel generally avoids figurative language, but there are a few exceptions: e.g., his comparison of "false infinity" to a straight line and "true infinity" to a circle (SL1, 164); and his extended simile contrasting calculus and philosophy with mathematics and natural history, and cavalierly comparing natural history to eating and drinking:

The principle of analysis of infinity is of a loftier nature than the principle of the mathematics of finite quantities; and so the [evidence appropriate to finite mathematics] has to be forsworn in calculus; just as philosophy cannot make any claim to the kind of "clarity" that the sciences of the sensory, like natural history, possess—and just as eating and drinking count as more understandable occupations than thinking and conceptualizing (SL1, 305).

In the Logic and the Philosophy of Spirit in the *Encyclopedia,* there is only an occasional use of metaphor. One of the most striking instances comes in the introduction to the section on "Phenomenology," where Hegel is developing the concept of the ego:

The ego is the lightning penetrating the natural soul and incinerating its naturalness. . . . The ego knows, and thus is consciousness. As this absolute negativity [of consciousness] it is in-itself the identity with its Other; The ego is itself this Other, and overreaches it object as something that is in-itself superseded. The ego is *one* side of the relationship, and the *whole* relationship—the *light* that manifests both itself and the other. . . . Just as the light is the manifestation of itself and its other (i.e., darkness), and can become manifest only by manifesting that other, so also is the ego only manifest insofar as its Other in the form of something independent from the ego is manifested (EIII, §§412-413 and Zusätze).

In the Philosophy of Nature, however, metaphorical language becomes pervasive. One must keep in mind that "philosophy of nature," an almost extinct philosophical discipline, is strongly distinguished— especially as understood in German idealism—from "natural philosophy," which emphasizes factual positivity; "philosophy of nature" is also distinct from "philosophy of science," which has an epistemological and methodological focus. Hegel's Philosophy of Nature deals systematically with the Idea in its state of *otherness* or alienation. Nature as a whole is an embodiment of the Idea, although the Idea is largely hidden, in some respects almost indiscernible, amid multiple contingencies and opacities. But since Nature embodies the Idea, one should not be surprised that frequent manifestations of the Idea (the harbinger of Spirit and consciousness) become manifest in spite of all the contingencies; and these manifestations give us constant evidence that Nature—even inorganic nature—is not, after all, "dead."

The natural phenomenon which seems to invite some of the most intense metaphorical treatment in the Philosophy of Nature is light.

Like the medieval scholastics Aquinas and Albertus Magnus, who associated light with a supraelemental "quintessence," Hegel attributes quasi-living qualities to light:

> Matter as immediate pure totality passes over into its opposite. . . . Matter as the restlessness of the whirlwind of this self-relating of matter to itself . . . is light. Light is the self-compressed totality of matter, but as pure force, as intensive self-possessing life. . . . Light is the pure self-reflection that in the higher form of Spirit is the ego. . . . Matter is heavy, insofar as it searches directly for local unity; but light is matter that has found itself (E2, §§275, 276).

Other aspects of matter lead to still other metaphorical descriptions. The impact of material bodies on one another is a "battle for a single space" (E2, §265, Zusatz); speed is the attempt of matter to approximate, as closely as possible, the self-movement of the Concept (E2, §267, Zusatz); sound is the mechanical soulfulness of a body, which expresses its ideality (E2, §300); the planet Earth is the "organic entity which assimilates the astral forces, which as heavenly bodies still have a semblance of independence, and brings them under the power of individuality; the Earth thus demotes these giant members of the larger universe to 'moments' of its own individuality" (E2, §280).

Probably the most anthropomorphic metaphors in Philosophy of Nature are to be found in Hegel's treatment of electricity:

> We regard electrical tension as the intrinsic selfhood of the physical totality of a body which maintains itself in its contact with another body. What we see is an upsurge of anger in the body; there is no one there but the body itself, least of all any alien matter. Its youthfulness breaks out, it raises itself on its hind legs; in opposing its connection with another its physical nature gathers its forces into the abstract ideality of light. It is not only we who compare bodies, for they compare themselves . . . (E2 §324, Zusatz).

Such a description—bodies comparing and contrasting themselves with other bodies, and sometimes breaking out into forceful reactions—would, of course, be considered poetry at best by contemporary scientists. But in a Philosophy of Nature, where an attempt is being made to trace the vestiges of Spirit and the earmarks of the Idea in physical phenomena, it might be considered an accurate portrayal of nature, not just a poetical flight of fancy. Much depends on whether one accepts the premise that there is indeed rationality, and implicitly Spirit, in inorganic as well as organic nature.

IV. Hegel's Paradoxes and Oxymorons: A Sampler

We have already seen that Hegel's later system as a whole is paradoxical—neither a subjective nor an objective set of categories, but focusing on subject-objects (like Being), allowing the negations of these objects to progress to positive determinations, and circling back at the end of the progressions to the point from which everything started. It should not be surprising that a system paradoxical in its very architectonic might generate numerous subsidiary paradoxes as it proceeds along its dialectical-speculative path. And so it does. As I have argued in a previous work,[7] it seems that dialectical procedures themselves, since they coordinate oppositions, tend to generate paradoxical propositions as their "solutions" or conclusions. Hegel's later system produces literally hundreds of paradoxical statements; and the alleged difficulty of reading Hegel is certainly in great part connected with the necessity of encountering paradox after paradox. Obviously, someone who equates paradox with bare contradiction would find Hegel's system impossible to comprehend—or even to read. But if one can get beyond that hurdle, reading Hegel becomes less formidable, and important philosophical insights begin to coalesce. Some examples follow

A. Metaphysical Paradoxes

Being is nothingness (SL1, 82ff; H1, §§39ff.; E1, §§84ff.): We talk about "beings" in a general way; but no one has ever seen Being itself. Still, everything—every being—is supposed to participate in Being. The concept Being is the result of abstraction from every determination. It is the complete absence of any determination. If it had any determination, such as (say) redness or heaviness, then as a consequence yellow things (say) or light things would not be beings. Thus every conceivable thing can be called a "being," simply because Being is so completely indeterminate itself.

But if Being is so completely lacking in every specific determination, it is nothingness. To see pure light, without any specific features or determinations, would be to see nothing; it would be tantamount to seeing pure darkness. Analogously, to think of Being without any further determination is to think of nothing; this is the same as thinking about nothingness. Being is the purest of abstractions, the product of thought, and in its pure abstract form it is indistinguishable from nothingness. Being and nothingness are just "two sides of the same coin"—complete absence of any specific determinations.

The true infinite comprises both finite and infinite (SL1, 149ff.; H1, §§47-48; E1, §§93-95): The infinity that we are most familiar with is mathematical infinity, a linear process in which a mathematical operation is carried out and an infinite process beyond a certain limit is indicated; for example, addition, as in 2, 4, 8, 10 . . . ∞, or squaring, as in 2, 4, 16, 256 . . . ∞. Calculus offers more complex examples of this process. But infinity is not confined to mathematics. It is also found in first-order reality. If a rock has a tendency to oxidize, this tendency impels it out of its finite determinations into the "beyond" of the alterations of oxidation; a seed is oriented toward reaching beyond its present state to blossom and flower; an animal is impelled continuously to throw off its present determinations as it activates its potentialities. This tendency of incessantly negating the finite in bringing out new aspects of the "in-itself" is found especially, of course, in human consciousness and the human spirit; and the chief example of this process is morality, which leads humans to negate natural inclinations for the sake of accomplishing duty, thus constantly transcending themselves. (Philosophers like Kant and Fichte have talked about an "infinite" progress unfolding as humans bring inclinations closer and closer to duty.)

In all these manifestations of infinity, it should be noticed that the finite itself is driven to go beyond its limits, to enter into infinity; but it should also be noticed that the infinite is outside the finite, requiring it, related to it, but also separate from it, and thus, in a sense, determinate. The infinite stands outside the finite, negating its negations; but the finite is also situated outside the infinite, showing that the infinite does not indeed encompass everything but is limited—at least by the finite which it attempts to transcend. And so we are confronted with an infinite finite, geared inexorably toward being transcended; and a finite infinite, never quite able to encompass that which it is passing beyond.

In order to grasp the *true* infinite, we have only to consider the circular interrelationship between finite and infinite that is evident in all of these examples. For example, in space we will never arrive at some limit beyond which there is no other limit—we will never arrive at an "edge of the universe." But if we get beyond this tedious process of setting limits and then surpassing them, we begin to see the infinite dynamic interrelationship between finite and infinite as the essential thing—and this is the true infinite. In the case of morality, the "ought" standing over against inclinations and tendencies is a false infinite: it is always there, right alongside the finite, and it can never be overcome, as Kant and Fichte realized; but the true infinite is the dynamic interrelationship between "is" and "ought," between the empirical ego, constitutionally oriented toward surpassing itself, and the ego "in itself," the ideal ego activating true potentialities rather than being frozen before unreal "oughts."

Identity is difference, and vice versa (SL2, 38ff.; H1, §§66-68; E1, §§115-18): Propositions of the form "A is B" have to be understood on two levels. On one level, they are stating an identity between A and B; but on the second level, identity patently implies that two different things are being identified. This is true of all statements with the copula "is" or an equivalent.

Even in our ordinary speech, we look for "identities in difference." If someone starts to say, for example, "A plant is . . . " or "Gold is . . . " or "God is . . . ," we are definitely and justifiably disappointed to hear "A plant is a plant" or "Gold is gold" or "God is God." These tedious tautologies add nothing to our knowledge and are especially obnoxious insofar as they purport to say something. The same considerations apply to the concept of identity, and to the logical "law of identity" which says that A is always identical with A:

> It is claimed that though the law of identity is unprovable, each and every consciousness proceeds according to this law, and as soon as we apprehend this law it coincides with our experience. But everyone's experience runs just opposite to this academic sort of assertion: Namely, no consciousness thinks or imagines or speaks along the lines of this "law," and *no* existent of any kind whatsoever exists according to this "law." Speech fashioned according to such a law of truth ("a planet is . . . a planet; magnetism is . . . magnetism; spirit is . . . spirit") is justifiably considered nonsensical (E1, §115).

Difference likewise cannot be taken as something abstract from or immune to identity. Difference is presumably identical with *itself*. If difference is *different* from identity, then "difference$_1$," which separates identity and difference, must be a different sort of difference from "difference$_2$," which it is separating.

The interconnection and inseparability of identity and difference become especially evident when we make comparisons in terms of "sim-

ilarity" and "difference." Similarity can be attributed only to things
which are in some way different, and the most interesting identities and
similarities are those found amid prima facie diversity; difference
requires a substratum—a common ground—which provides the basis
for comparison. The empirical sciences offer ample evidence that an
explicit connection between difference and identity is the general rule.
In physics, for example, there is a constant search for new elements, new
forces, new genera; and there are constant attempts to show that bodies
which were previously considered simple are in reality quite complex.
This thrust toward diversification is counterbalanced, however, by an
equally constant attempt to show unities where only differences have so
far been seen—e.g., unifying chemical reactions and electricity, or
reducing the organic processes of nutrition to chemical processes.

*"The rational is the real and the real is the rational" (PSK, §233ff.; SL2,
200ff.; PR, 24-26; E1, §§6, 142ff.):* Hegel made this observation at the
outset of his *Rechtsphilosophie* (1821),[8] and it provoked much consterna-
tion from his critics. Toward the beginning of the 1830 edition of the
Encyclopedia he reiterates his position on the rationality of reality, and
then takes the opportunity to reply to his critics:

> Those earlier remarks [in the *Rechtsphilosophie*] astonished many and
> elicited hostility, even among people who do not want to be at odds with
> philosophy or religion. It is superfluous to cite Religion in this regard,
> since the doctrines of religion about divine providence express these prin-
> ciples [of the rationality of reality] all too emphatically. As regards the
> philosophical implications, we must presuppose enough philosophical
> sophistication to realize not only that God is real, but that He is the most
> real, that He alone is truly real, but also, if we would be precise, that in
> general existence is partly *appearance* and only partly reality. In ordinary
> life a person capriciously names every chance happening and error and
> evil—and, for that matter, every trivial and transitory existent—a "real-
> ity." But even for ordinary sensibility a contingent existence will not
> merit the unambiguous title of "a reality" (PR, §6).

Hegel's reference to religion, and by implication to the doctrine of
divine providence, is instructive. A theologian challenged by a skeptic
about all the negative and evil and trivial things happening in the world
might answer, "But this is not what is *really* going on. God writes
straight with crooked lines"—or something to that effect. The point of
such an answer would be that a providential plan is working itself out,

often imperceptibly, amid apparently unprovidential events. Similarly, a philosopher might want to reserve the appellation "real" for a certain subset of events or things that are judged "really real" according to some criterion. For Hegel, the criterion is rationality.

Reason in Hegel's system is a "both-and"; this contrasts with the "either-or" of the Understanding. It is a technical term for the comprehensive grasp of oppositions—subject-object, inner-outer, etc. It is that which manifests a *correspondence between* objectivity and the conceptual-ideal.

There are experiential grounds for maintaining that the rational, in this sense, is the real. A statesman who does not conform to the commonly held ideal of a statesman (and perhaps not even to his own ideal) is not a real statesman. If a musician's performance does not conform to our concept of music, we may say that he or she is "not a real musician." If a plan or a strategy or a moral objective is developed which does not take into account relevant facts, it is "unrealizable," not a "real" plan or strategy or objective. If a state claims to be a democracy but falls far short of respecting individual rights, it may be judged not to be a "real" democracy. In Hegel's Philosophy of Nature, a higher level of rationality-reality will be ascribed to phenomena like magnetism and organic life, in which the closeness of reality to Reason or the Idea is most evident. In his political philosophy—the source of the controversial statement mentioned above—it is essential to search out the truly rational elements in the modern state; in Hegel's framework, this is especially the coordination of nature and Spirit. Conversely, the "realities" of the state, from a philosophical point of view, will be the rational elements which have already been incorporated constitutionally, or in policy, and so on.

Some expressions in modern philosophy throw light on Hegel's general position in this regard. In Sartrean existentialism, for example, those who do not give expression to their freedom are called "inauthentic"; in other words, they manifest a species of unreality. In political philosophy the rather pejorative term *realpolitik* is often used to designate political structures which abandon ideals and the ideal to concentrate on power games. (Actually, this kind of abandonment would lead for Hegel to "unrealpolitik"; critics who associate Hegel's paradox with realpolitik are missing his point.)

Logico-metaphysical oxymorons: Occasionally, the dialectical developments in Hegel's Logic are summed up briskly in oxymorons, sometimes multiple oxymorons. For example, *essence* considered in its abstractness is an "external inner," an inessential essence—i.e., the mere appearance of essence (H1, §§89-90; E1, §140). Similarly, "possibility" is an inessential essentiality, an external "inner"; and since the opposite of possibility, not being an actuality, is worth just as much as possibility, every possibility is at the same time an impossibility (H1, §92; E1, §143). As we shall see, Hegel resorts to oxymorons even more frequently in *Realphilosophie,* in the philosophies of Nature and Spirit.

B. Cosmological Paradoxes:

Nature is the Idea in a state of transition (E2, §§247-51): The eternal and timeless Idea in its containment of opposition is the epitome of internalized superseded negativity. But this internalization is also superseded, and the result of the supersession is Nature. Nature is the ultimate manifestation of the Idea in its *exteriority;* actually, it would be more precise to speak about Nature as the Idea in a state of its own exteriority to itself. Nature is the "trash heap" (*Abfall*) of the Idea. But it contains incredible riches—as the castoffs of a fabulously wealthy person might contain treasures. On the whole, it is something like a bacchanalian god:

> In Christ the contradiction [between universality and individuality] is established and superseded, in his life, passion and resurrection. Nature [on the other hand] is God's son—but not as the Son, but like a crystallization in exteriority—the divine Idea as held fast outside of [divine] love for the moment. Nature is self-alienated Spirit, a Spirit which is *set loose* in nature, a bacchanalian god, uninhibited and unbridled; in Nature the unity of the Concept is hidden. . . . Nature is the Idea only in-itself; hence Schelling calls it a "petrified" intelligence, others speak of a "frozen" intelligence. But God does not abide in Nature petrified and dead. Rather, the stones cry out and elevate themselves to Spirit (E2, §247).

Thus we are right to stand in awe of Nature and its wonders. But we must keep in mind that Nature in itself is not divine, not to be worshipped. Nature and Spirit are still worlds apart. The Concept is only latent in Nature's interior, weighted down with multiple contingencies and opacities. Even the triadic development of the Idea from universality to particularity to individuality is obscured in Nature, since the second moment of particularity characteristically bifurcates, leading to polarities, and resulting in overall tetradic developments. But the vestiges of Spirit and life are still pervasive throughout Nature and give rise to stages of development in which Nature gradually approaches its truth. Thus there is a progression to vegetative and animal life, and ultimately to consciousness. This is to be understood, however, not as biological evolution but as progressive concretions of initially abstract matter to its ultimate concretion in Spirit, a progression of finite objects which create time in and through their movements and changes.

Cosmological oxymorons: Hegel's Philosophy of Nature is concerned largely with exploring the vestiges of the Idea in Nature and elaborating the conceptual gradations of the approach to Spirit in Nature. If this is a viable enterprise, one should, in the first place, not expect the sort of mathematical rigor associated, for example, with experimental physics. But in view of Hegel's premise that the Idea/Spirit is largely encumbered by contingencies and contradictions in many stages of Nature, and that it often expresses its antitheses in polarities, we should not be surprised at the proliferation of oxymorons to express the various stages. Oxymorons indeed appear here more frequently than in any other part of Hegel's system. As they verbally compress opposed or contradictory elements, they give an impression of the ongoing struggles of the system of nature to manifest the Spirit that is at its core. At times they border on poetry, but they differ from poetry in that they appear as the upshot of sustained argument—as concluding formulations that attempt to tie up some of the points in a neat phrase. Some examples follow.

Space is not the subjective form of intuition that Kant hypothesized; on the contrary, it is pure, abstract, quality-less, quantitative, mutual externality, connecting isolated points three-dimensionally in an endless succession. As such, it is a "unity in externality," an "undifferentiated difference," a "unity of discreteness and continuity," an "insensible sensorium" or "sensory insensibility," not only an external determination but "intrinsic externality" (E2, §§254-55).

Time is not distinct from space. It is the aspect of the "insensible sensorium" of space wherein spatial indifferent-differences negate their negation and arrive at something like an abstract counterpart of the ego's self-identity. In time we intuit "becoming itself"; thus its characteristics are analogous to those of "becoming." Time "exists insofar as it does not exist," and "is nonexistent insofar as it exists"; although everything is in time, time terminates in a "now" which comes from the nothingness of the past and inexorably recedes into the nothingness of the future. Thus its inclusiveness is exclusive and its omnipotence is power-lessness (E2, §247, Zusatz; §§257-58).

Matter is the pure unity of "form" accruing to all the diversification of the Idea in Nature; in matter, the necessities of the Idea are expressed as contingencies (E2, §§262, 265; 308, Zusatz).

Gravity is the Concept attaching to the "Conceptlessness" of matter, the interiority of that which has no interior (E2, §262).

Light (*Licht*), in contrast to gravity, is the "absolutely light" (*leicht*), a "material ideality," a "relationless relation in-itself," "immaterial mat-ter." In contrast to the repose of matter, light is also "absolute speed"; and if the astronomers are right in their conjecture that the light of the stars reaches us after many eons, then light is also the joining of the past and present (E2, §§275, Zusatz; 276).

Force is an infinity which is always embodied in a finite, determinate content (H2, §85).

As we proceed further into the determinations of physical objects, we find that *elasticity* is the subsistence-nonsubsistence of atoms and mole-cules, an intensive-extensive quantum (E2, §299); that *sound* is the tran-sition of spatiality into temporality (E2, §300); that *heat* is a "physical configuration freeing itself from configuration" (E2, §307); that the *crys-tal* is a circularity with sides, an extended pointedness (E2, §315); and so forth.

C. Paradoxes in Consciousness and Spirit:

Exclusive particulars are universal and inclusive (E3, §419, Zusatz): In sen-sory consciousness we have the impression that we are encountering iso-lated, distinct particulars. But these "particulars" have common features with other particulars and ultimately share the characteristic of being particular; thus they are universal. Also, while they seem to exclude other particulars, they simultaneously set up relationships to the others, become dependent on these relationships for their "exclusivity," and are actually mediated through these relationships.

Absolute freedom determines itself to be determined (PR, §§26-30): Freedom which remains in a state of abstract subjectivity, priding itself on its "free choice," is, because of its incompleteness, merely a caricature of free-dom. Freedom has a necessary thrust toward objectifying itself; and this means that it must build up around itself all the objective accouter-ments that bolster freedom, and, when they are at their most effective, almost make it impossible not to be free. In other words, freedom needs the bulwark of morality, a system of right and laws, and ultimately a constitutional government. In order to ensure maximum self-determination for all individuals, these individuals must be determined objectively and externally to exercise self-determination.

Morality can only be achieved through social and political relationships (PR, §§129-41): In modern philosophy, since Kant, we tend to think of morality in terms of subjectively construed duties to ourselves and to others. One can easily conceive of a morality which is private, personal, and apolitical. But the concept of duties to ourselves implies a consciousness of otherness within ourselves, and ultimately the intersubjective consciousness of other selves. And the concept of duties to others can be meaningful only in the context of an objective set of rights and duties. The moral conscience as a subjective attempt to coordinate and harmonize rights and duties both engenders and is derived from the objective coordination of rights and duties in the social and political spheres. The interrelationship of conscience and this objective sphere constitutes "moral good" in the ultimate sense.

Democracy is an impediment to the highest political freedom (PR, §308; E3, §544): Hegel was a strong advocate of the "modern free state" as a final stage in the explicit political recognition of individual subjectivity; but he held that democracy, often considered to be the final guarantee of individual liberty, did not go far enough. The problem with democracy, in Hegel's view, is that it holds to an overly abstract idea of individual input and influence on government, and it lacks the precise mediating agencies which are necessary to facilitate that input and influence:

> There is a prevailing idea that *all* individuals should participate in the deliberations and decisions concerning general governmental concerns, since they are all members of the state and state concerns are the concerns of *all,* and all have a *right* to be present with their knowledge and volition in these deliberations. This idea, which would like to install the *democratic* element *without any rational form* in the state-organism (which can only exist as such with this rational form) gets our attention because it insists on the *abstract* determination of being a member of the state; and superficial thinking remains on the level of abstractions. . . . [But] the concrete state is the *totality distributed through its component social circles;* a member of a state is a *member* of such *social divisions;* and only in this objective determination can the individual come into consideration in the state (PR §308).

The social divisions that Hegel has in mind include not only the various classes of society (business class, agricultural class, etc.) but also *Corporationen* (labor unions, professional societies, religious bodies, etc.). Hegel's idea is that in reality, an individual's primary influence is through the various groupings with which he or she is affiliated, and the individual can have a meaningful impact on government only through them. The key idea here is that a government, according to its Concept, is *organic;* and just as individual cells function in a body only through the organs through which they are differentiated, so also individuals in the "body politic" need mediation through election of the delegates and representatives of their respective groupings or classes. A strict democratic approach which insisted on "one man, one vote" would lead to an unmanageable dispersion and dilution of the individual's vote rather than political empowerment (PR §308; E3 §544).

Chapter Five

Hegel's Perspective
on Other Philosophers

Hegel's treatment of the history of philosophy has to be understood in the context of his rather remarkable theory that there is, indeed, only one system of philosophy, evolving ineluctably in history. Although various philosophical "systems" with their various principles (or lack of principles) appear historically, there is only one philosophical system. It is the duty of philosophy to differentiate and discriminate between these "systems" (H1, §8). None of them is to be discounted out of hand; they all are necessary stages in philosophical development, although some are of interest primarily for exemplifying untenable extremes. Looking back over all these endeavors, Hegel concludes that the history of philosophy—understood *philosophically*—is a pantheon of moments in the development of eternal truth (E1, §86, Zusatz).

It is obvious that Hegel has a rather sublime, and perhaps unparalleled, concept of philosophy and the vocation of philosophers. Although philosophers may seem isolated from one another in space, time, or both, they are all contributing to the single system of philosophy. Their history cannot just be a chronicle of who said what when, who influenced whom, whether there were agreements or disagreements, etc. Rather, as Hegel views it, their history is more precisely a story—with characters and motivations and goals, and the equivalent of a plot. The story has to do with the development of the "identity in difference" of being and thought; and philosophers, as protagonists or antagonists in this story, have always been concerned, consciously or unintentionally, with the accomplishment of this purpose.

If we judge from his emphases and his explicit treatment of philosophers, Hegel apparently thought that this story took place primarily in western civilization—eastern philosophies "marched to a different drummer." Hegel passed over "oriental philosophies" very quickly in his *Lectures on the History of Philosophy.* Because of their identification with eastern religions, they simply are not on the same level as western philosophies, which have been traditionally distinct from religion (HP1,

138). Chinese and Indian philosophy do receive some attention from Hegel; but his treatment is perfunctory and highly critical (HP1, 138ff.). In any case, there had been no significant cross-fertilization of western and eastern philosophies up to Hegel's time.

I. Ancient Greek Philosophy

The "story" of philosophy, then, begins with a quest, in western civilization, for determining the relationship of being to thought. Parmenides poses the question explicitly, and sets the parameters of the challenge for subsequent generations of philosophers, when he says:

> Thinking and the object of thought are the same. For you will not find thought apart from being, nor either of them apart from utterance. Indeed, there is not anything at all apart from being. . . .[1]

Since Parmenides was the first to differentiate Being from sense objects and explicitly bring out its relationship to thought, the history of philosophy properly begins with him. Hegel quotes the above passage in his own translation and observes:

> This is the main idea in Parmenides. Thinking produces itself; what is produced is a thought; thus thinking is identical with Being, since there is nothing outside of this great affirmation, Being. . . . Genuine philosophizing begins with Parmenides. One can see in this text the movement into the higher plane of the Ideal. A single man frees himself from all representations and opinions, disputes their "truth," and says, "Only the necessary, only Being is what is true" (HP1, 290).

But this is only the beginning. Parmenides set up the problematic, and Zeno and other Eleatics and the Pythagoreans made some inroads; but they were prevented from making further progress because they confined themselves to the either-or approach of the Understanding. The real breakthrough—out of the standpoint of the Understanding to true speculative thought—arrived only with Heraclitus. Heraclitus not only paved the way for further development of the being-thought problematic but supplied us with the paradigm for speculative philosophizing:

> With Heraclitus the philosophical Idea comes to the fore for the first time in its speculative form. The discursive thought of Parmenides and

Zeno is abstract Understanding. Heraclitus was celebrated (and also derogated) as a profound philosopher. Here we catch a sight of land. There is no principle of Heraclitus that I have not incorporated into my Logic (HP1, 320).

Zeno before Heraclitus had comprehended dialectic in its negative aspects and generated subjective antitheses or "paradoxes." But this was bare dialectic. The great advance of Heraclitus over Zeno was to grasp dialectic in its positive, speculative aspects, and as a λόγος encompassing objectivity:

> This audacious spirit [Heraclitus] was the first to give expression to the profound saying, "Being is not something over and above nonbeing." In other words, Being and Nothingness are identical; the essential thing is *change*. The truth is just the unity of opposites. With the Eleactics, we had merely the abstract Understanding that only Being exists. We [in modern philosophy] replace Heraclitus's formulation with: "The Absolute is the unity of Being and nonbeing.". . . . This is a grand idea— the transition from Being to Becoming. It is still abstract; but, in another sense, it is also the first concrete, the first unity of opposed determinations (HP1, 324–25).

Heraclitus, in his dialectic, is thus seen as the forerunner of the concrete unity of opposites. Plato and Aristotle developed this theme even further and arrived at speculative philosophy—idealism in the modern sense (HP2, 133). But although Plato arrived at the Idea with an abstract affirmation of the reality of the ideal, Aristotle surpassed him by bringing out the full negativity prevailing in the self-identity of the Idea (HP2, 155; H1, §139). The Idea becomes especially concrete in Aristotle's theory of God's nature as "self-thinking thought" (HP2, 247). But neither Plato nor Aristotle was able to develop his admittedly speculative philosophy into a *system:*

> One can talk about a Platonic or Aristotelian "system"; but their philosophies were not in the form of a system. In order to be a system, a *single* principle would have to be expounded and developed consistently through all the particulars (HP2, 246).

In other words, if Aristotle, for example, were to produce a philosophical system, he would have to show how his ultimate principle, God as "self-thinking thought," is related to all the categories of reality. But philosophical speculation was not developed sufficiently among the ancient Greeks for such a project to be undertaken.

II. The Middle Ages

In Hegel's opinion, the domination of the Catholic Church during the Middle Ages was detrimental to the progress of philosophy. Theology flourished, and it was genuinely philosophical—providing a model for post-Reformation theology, which had become largely opposed to any semblance of philosophical speculation.[2] But philosophy itself, in particular Scholasticism, burdened with ecclesiastical demands and expectations, lacked the intellectual climate necessary for independent progress (HP3BS, 48–49).

Hegel's dim view of medieval philosophizing is reflected, in HP2, in his extremely short, curt treatment of thinkers who would now be classified as major Scholastics. For example, Thomas Aquinas and John Duns Scotus receive only a few paragraphs apiece; and the entire section on several centuries of Scholasticism runs only a small fraction of the length he devotes to either ancient or modern philosophy.

One exception is Anselm—a Scholastic who receives serious attention from Hegel, and a little more space. What Hegel finds of interest is Anselm's "ontological proof" of the existence of God, which argues from the concept of God to God's existence. This proof was considered invalid by Aquinas and was an object of trenchant criticism by Kant and many others in Hegel's day (it is still a subject of dispute in our own day). But in Hegel's eyes it contained an immensely important, pathbreaking speculative insight:

> With Anselm . . . the opposition between thought itself and Being—this infinite extreme—comes to the fore. This pure abstraction, which first came to consciousness within Christendom, this bifurcation as such, was established and perpetuated in the Middle Ages. As in an imaginative representation, here for the first time the Concept and Being appear in opposition; and their connection is being attempted [by Anselm]. . . . The unity of Being and Thought is the genuine content that Anselm had in mind, but in the form of [discursive] Understanding. The two poles are identical only via a third determination—Anselm's "highest thinkable concept"—to which they are compared as to an external standard of measurement (HP2, 555, 558).

But while Anselm's contribution to speculative philosophy is undeniable, it still leaves something to be desired. For the unity of subject and object presupposed in Anselm's "ontological proof" is something merely subjective and implicit (E1, §193); the distinction between subject and object is still paramount, even in the formulation of the proof. It is true that for the God we conceptualize to be perfect, he must have "existence." But there is a decisive difference between finite existence, which implies a disparity between concept and existence, and God's existence, which implies just the opposite. By definition, God's existence implies the unity of concept and existence. The idea of God is the infinite unity-in-distinction, in which being and thought entail each other in the same way that body and soul entail each other. Anselm himself realized this intuitively, though he did not bring out the relationship explicitly.

The post-Anselm task has thus become clear. What has to be done is to take Anselm's positive insight and bring out the negativity or negative interrelationships of the moments in that insight (H1, §139). To progress beyond Anselm, new approaches to Parmedides' problematic of the identity of thought and being are needed.

III. Modern Philosophy

According to Hegel, Descartes's *Cogito, ergo sum* provided a major breakthrough. In sharp contrast with Parmenides, who finds thought immanent in being, Descartes discovers being immanent in thought. A completely new philosophical horizon has begun to be opened up.

Descartes and the Cartesians made two extremely important contributions to all subsequent philosophers. First, they emphasized subjectivity and thinking—a shift in emphasis which laid the groundwork for modern philosophy. Second, they made explicit what had been only implicit in previous speculative philosophers: for although Aristotle, Plato, and others had arrived at the insight—the identity of subjectivity and objectivity (S/0)—it was René Descartes, Baruch Spinoza, and others who actually stated this understanding (H1, 139).

As noted above, this new perspective opened up new horizons, and it made possible some important philosophical accomplishments. For example, on the basis of the new, explicit understanding of the unity of thought and existence, Descartes presented his own version of something like an "ontological proof" of God's existence, and also extended the implications of the proof to questions about the "connection" between body and soul (SL2, 402; E3, 389 and Zusatz).

The Cartesians moved in divergent philosophical directions but still adhered to, and advanced, Descartes's basic insight. Spinoza made the identity of thought and being axiomatic in his system (H1, §139); he was hampered, however, by his own zeal for the synthetic method, which is appropriate for geometry but counterproductive in philosophy (E1, §§229, 231). Gottfried Leibniz likewise was hampered methodologically—he started out unphilosophically with a "hypothesis," as if he were a physicist, and then looked for experimental confirmation (HP3, 237)—but he at least counterbalanced Spinoza's monistic, synthetic extremes by affirming individuality (HP3, 255; E1, §151 and Zusatz). Leibniz should also be credited for showing that external differentiation is intimately connected with and derived from the specific difference inherent *within* things (E1, §117).

Not unexpectedly, the Cartesian shift in emphasis led to subjectivist extremes, such as an overemphasis on having "clear and distinct ideas"—a merely psychological characterization without any significant philosophical import (H1, §114). And English philosophers like John Locke, in their own search for clear ideas and their quasi-empirical focus on subjectivity, ended up in prephilosophical "blind alleys" and detours by trying to use a hybrid analytic method unsuited to philosophy (E1, §227). Subsequently, the "critical philosophy" of Immanuel Kant also fell prey to this overemphasis on subjectivity.

But—Hegel is careful to add—this should not blind us to the monumental categorial revolution that took place with the publication of Kant's *Critique of Pure Reason.* If we compare Kant's twelve categories with Aristotle's ten categories (or "predicaments"), we can get an idea of the tremendous movement that has taken place in philosophy in recent years:

> The Category, which formerly had the connotation of being the substantiality of what exists—either (indefinitely) the substantiality of existence-in-general, or the substantiality of existence over against consciousness—is now the substantiality, that is, the simple unity, of the existent only insofar as it is a *thinking-reality* (PSK, §235).

In other words, whereas in the aftermath of Aristotelian metaphysics consciousness strove to conform to the substantiality of existence, with the Kantian revolution substantial existence is tested for conformity to thought categories.

This was an important development, since it finally drew attention to the contributions of subjectivity to so-called "objective" knowledge. But we should keep in mind that Kant's main contribution was not philosophical but strictly *phenomenological;* it only laid the groundwork for further progress in philosophy.

The Kantian "philosophy" can at best be characterized as apprehending Spirit in the form of consciousness and thus as bearing the earmarks of phenomenology—not of philosophy proper. Kantianism considers the *ego* as a relationship to something lying "beyond," which in its most abstract determination is called a "thing-in-itself " . . . (E3, §415).

Actually, toward the end of his Third Critique, the *Critique of Judgment,* Kant himself almost managed to proceed from phenomenology to true speculative philosophy, but he unfortunately failed to realize the significance of the insight he had chanced on. He missed the opportunity that opened up before him:

> When Kant's Third Critique in the concept of *reflective* judgment arrives at the *Idea* of Spirit, the Subject-Objectivity, an *intuitive Understanding,* etc., and also comes to the Idea of Nature—the Idea in these cases is merely counted as an "appearance," in other words, the Idea is demoted to a subjective "maxim" (E3, §415; see also E1, §58).

Johann Gottlieb Fichte was aware of Kant's phenomenological impasse and tried to bridge the gap between ego and non-ego in his own transcendental system. But he was never quite able to free himself from Kantian subjectivism:

> The Fichtean philosophy had the same standpoint as Kant's philosophy, and Fichte's "non-ego" is merely determined as the *object* of the ego, merely determined within *consciousness*. This non-ego persists as an infinite "stoking" [*Anstoß*], i.e. a thing-in-itself. Both philosophers demonstrate in this way that they have not arrived at the *Concept* nor at *Spirit* as it exists in-and-for-itself. Rather, they have attained to Spirit only in its relationship-to-another [the phenomenological standpoint] (E3, §415).

The rapid changes taking place in speculative philosophy eventually came to a climax in Schelling's *Naturphilosophie*. Schelling begins with the Fichtean identity of ego and non-ego (HP3, 430) but then forges ahead, well beyond subjectivism to the true absolute standpoint (HP3, 315, 364). Thus the trio of Kant, Fichte, and Schelling—in concert— have laid the groundwork for true speculative philosophy.

> The philosophies of Kant, Fichte and Schelling: It is in these philosophies that the revolution in the style of thinking, to which the modern Spirit has progressed in Germany, has been established and expressed. The succession of these three philosophers embodies the path which thought has

followed. . . . The *Kantian* philosophy first of all set forth the formal aspects of the task, but had as its result merely the abstract absoluteness of reason in self-consciousness . . . ; next in succession came the *Fichtean* philosophy, which grasped the essence of self-consciousness speculatively as concrete I-ness [*Ichheit*], but did not get beyond this subjective form of the Absolute. *Schelling's* philosophy then proceeds from this viewpoint, casts it aside, and proposes the Idea of the Absolute, that which is true in-and-for-itself (HP3, 314–15).

Hegel himself takes his starting point from, and finds a mentor in, Schelling—who, in a living, contemporary dialectic, had brought these philosophical developments to their natural conclusion. Hegel is critical of Schelling on many points, but in his *Lectures on the History of Philosophy,* the last of which are on Schelling, he concludes with high praise for Schelling's final contributions to the "philosophical revolution":

> Schelling's philosophy is the final interesting philosophical form which we have had to consider. The Idea itself was brought out into the open: the true is the concrete, the unity of objective and subjective. . . . The principal contribution in Schelling's philosophy is that it has to do with a content, with the true; and the true is grasped as concrete. Schellingian philosophy has a deep speculative content; a content which, as content, is just what the whole history of philosophy has been concerned with. Thought is free for-itself, but in itself concrete, and not abstract; thought comprehends itself as world, but intellectual-real world, and not mere intellectual world (HP3, 453–54).

But Schelling, in trying to avoid Fichte's subjectivism, unfortunately went to the opposite extreme. As Hegel puts it in *The Difference between Fichte's and Schelling's System of Philosophy,* Schelling proposes an "objective subject-object" instead of a "subjective subject-object" (DFS, 12)—but these are equally unsatisfactory alternatives. And Schelling's solution was rendered even more problematic because, instead of trying to justify his "principle of absolute identity" philosophically, he depended almost entirely on intuition. Toward the end of the *Phenomenology of Spirit,* Hegel describes Fichte's and Schelling's alternatives as a choice between exaggerated egocentrism and arbitrary mystical immersion in substantiality. For Fichte, discerning the absolute principle involves the

> withdrawal of self-consciousness into its pure inwardness . . . [not realizing that] the ego in the *form* of *self-consciousness* does not have to hold itself

fast against the form of substantiality and objectivity, as if it had anxiety about being externalized (PSK, §804).

For Schelling, discerning the absolute principle is the

> mere absorption of self-consciousness into substance and the nonexistence of self-consciousness's differentiation . . . [so that the ego] is some mediating entity that casts the differences back into the abyss of the absolute and asserts their "identity" within the absolute (PSK, §804).

Hegel offers his services as a mediator in this apparent impasse. He proposes an absolute standpoint which (1) will overcome the Kantian rift between the transcendental ego and the thing-in-itself; (2) will be a privileged position in which subjectivity and objectivity coincide; but (3) unlike Schelling's approach, will depend not on intuition but on a systematic proof in which the negative relationships between subjectivity and objectivity are demonstrated to mediate the "immediate" intuition. At the conclusion of the *Phenomenology of Spirit,* Hegel maintains that the work has accomplished this purpose of completing the demonstration that Fichte and Schelling left unfinished:

> Spirit has shown us that it is *the very movement* of **self** which [a] externalizes itself from itself and sinks itself into its substance, **and** moreover [b] as subject is gone out of this substance into itself, **and** [c] makes substance into object and content, while it [the movement of spirit] supersedes this latter differentiation of objectivity and content. . . . The power of spirit is to remain self-identical **amid** its externalization and, as the existence-in-and-for-self, to posit **existence-for-self** merely as a moment, in the same way that it posits *existence-in-self.* . . . Knowledge consists in this apparent inactivity [of Spirit] that merely considers how what is differentiated moves itself in itself and devolves once again into its unity (PSK, §804).

The "apparently inactive" knowledge referred to here is *Absolute Knowledge*—"absolute" both in the sense that it coordinates subjective and objective aspects (subject and substance) and keeps them in equipoise, and in the sense that it is knowledge of the Absolute Idea. In ordinary speech, a distinction is made between knowledge and the object of knowledge; but here that distinction is no longer meaningful. Since in Hegel's usage the Idea is not some abstraction formulated by a consciousness but explicitly incorporates consciousness and the subjective knowing which gives rise to it, Absolute Knowledge is the same as the Absolute Idea. Thus when Hösle maintains that the Idea in the final sections of Hegel's Logic is the kernel of the entire system, which the initial stages of the Logic presupposed, and to which (at least as Hegel intended) the Philosophies of Nature and Spirit were meant to correspond, the same could be said about Absolute Knowledge. The Idea/Absolute Knowledge is Hegel's revised and (in his eyes) fully mediated version of Kant's seminal insight about "intellectual intuition," Fichte's principle of "ego and non-ego," and Schelling's speculation about an "absolute subject-object" or "absolute indifference."

At the end of his lectures on the history of philosophy, Hegel sums up the post-Schelling situation for his students:

> Pure thought has progressed to the opposition of the *Subjective* and the *Objective;* and the genuine reconciliation of this opposition is the insight that the opposition, driven to its absolute culmination, is dissolved in itself. As Schelling says, opposed things are identical; and they are not only identical in themselves, but eternal life consists precisely in eternally reproducing the opposition and eternally reconciling it.—Knowing opposition in unity, and unity in opposition is what *Absolute Knowledge* is all about; and Science is the knowledge of this unity in its entire self-unfolding development. . . . This, then, is where we stand in the present era, and the series of spiritual configurations has been brought to a close for the time being. (HP3, 459–61)

Hegel then goes on to reemphasize his theory that there is in reality only one system of philosophy:

> Here is the overall result of the history of philosophy: 1. Throughout all time there has been only *one* philosophy, whose concurrent differences bring out the necessary aspects of their *single* principle; 2. the succession of philosophical systems is nothing contingent, but exhibits the necessary series of stages of the development of this Science; 3. the final philosophy of any era is the result of the aforesaid development, and constitutes the truth in the highest configuration that the self-consciousness of Spirit appropriates concerning itself. Hence the final philosophy encompasses those that preceded, comprises all the stages in itself, and is the product and result of all its predecessors. (HP3, 461)

It goes without saying that Hegel thought his own "system" brought to a spiritual culmination all the crisscrossing currents of previous stages in the history of philosophy; thus it was the "highest point" that the "one system" of philosophy had reached. This implies a humble indebtedness along with a sense of being in a privileged position. But does it leave room for further progress? From Hegel's era to our own, allegations have been made that Hegel thought that he himself had brought philosophy to its *final* culmination—that philosophy had in some sense ended with his own philosophy. But Hegel never makes such a claim; in fact, in the passage above he makes the general observation that "the final philosophy in any era" is a culmination of all previous currents. The statement as it stands applies to future as well as past eras, and thus connotes a relative rather than an absolute "culmination." And we have no reason to look for hidden meanings in Hegel's statement (in the summation quoted earlier) that "the series of spiritual configurations has been brought to a close for the time being." There is no evidence that Hegel thought his system was the "last word"; and, as Hösle observes, Hegel even offers us good reasons for *not* being Hegelians:

> One who adheres to Hegel's idea of a type of absolute, ontological, transcendental philosophy does not on that account become a "Hegelian." An uncritical adherence to Hegel 150 years after his death is clearly impossible. This conclusion follows from basic convictions of Hegel himself—his thesis concerning [philosophical] progress. He says [HP1, 65]: "Because of [the relation of a philosophy to its historical era] there can be no contemporary Platonists, no Aristotelians, no Stoics or Epicureans. To resuscitate [these systems] means being willing to bring Spirit in its more sophisticated and profounder form to an earlier stage of development. This could never be satisfactory." What this observation signifies for our own time is this: There may be philosophers who attempt to mediate the tradition of objective idealism from Plato to Hegel with the post-Hegelian philosophy and contemporary science; but there can be no more Hegelians (Hösle 1988, 57 and note).

If, as Hegel maintains, both political forms (PR, 26) and philosophical systems (HP3, 456) are products of their own time and cannot transcend this temporal conditioning, one may also have second thoughts about being a Hegelian even in regard to his theory of the necessary progression of philosophical systems. This theory was also a product of its time. Certainly Hegel was conditioned by the section on "Epochs" in Schelling's *System of Transcendental Idealism* and by other contemporary theories about necessary stages in the progressive development of human consciousness, as well as by the all-pervasive Enlightenment notions about unending human progress. These influences certainly might lead one to look for a kind of organic progress in philosophical thinking. In our own time, influenced as we are by Darwin's theory of "natural selection" and by a general skepticism about intrinsic teleology in any sphere, as well as by antisystems and nonsystems that disclaim all relationships to predecessors, it is difficult to take Hegel's thesis seriously. But Hegel's guiding idea—that in the history of philosophy there has been, and still is, a continual wrestling with the subject-object problematic—has many prima facie verifications, even in contemporary philosophy, in questions about hermeneutical circles, nonfoundational epistemologies, the applicability of the quantum-mechanical principle of indeterminacy to metaphysics, etc. And progress is still possible on Kant's problem of the thing-in-itself. We must be careful not to "throw out the baby with the bathwater"—not to discard the valid and crucial problematic along with the time-bound methodology.

Chapter Six

Pivotal Themes and Hegelian Perspectives

I. The Future of Metaphysics

Hegel's *Phenomenology of Spirit* has been called a "metaphysics of consciousness"; and the *Science of Logic* and the Logic in the *Encyclopedia* are often referred to as his "metaphysics." But qualifications are needed when we speak of Hegel's "metaphysics." On the one hand, he is thoroughly a product of the Kantian reform and revision of metaphysics (which amounted to a revolution); on the other hand, he moves beyond Kant to reestablish some of the approaches and concentrations of traditional pre-Kantian metaphysics. The nuances of his position can be clarified by examining some highlights of the evolution of metaphysics in western philosophy:

A. Aristotle and First Philosophy

Aristotle's intention of investigating "first philosophy," later called "metaphysics," is initially announced in his *Physics*. The *Physics* is concerned primarily with physical substances and their forms, and the analysis of changes and interactions among them. "First philosophy," Aristotle promises, will go further and make an "accurate determination of the first principle in respect to form, whether it is one or many and what it is or what they are."[1] In the *Physics,* the world is viewed as a myriad of substances and substantial forms, which presuppose some type of material substrata—some substrata being closer to certain forms than to others. So *meta*physics, in Aristotle's system, is concerned with distinguishing the various types of substances, grading them in terms of the actuality of their form, speculating about the existence and nature of incorporeal substances, showing the relationship of form to matter in individual corporeal substances, showing how the forms are generated and altered and how bodies are moved, classifying substances into genera and species, etc.

Aristotle actually begins to carry out some of these objectives in the *Physics* itself, even speculating at length about a "prime mover" as the ultimate cause of all motion and change. But his explicit examination of the ultimate unmoved and separate causes of physical reality is officially relegated to the "first science," *Metaphysics:*

> The first science deals with things which both exist separately [like the objects of physics] and are immovable [like the objects of mathematics]. . . . If there is an immovable substance, the science of this must be prior and must be first philosophy, and universal in this way, because it is first.[2]

Aristotle's *Metaphysics* is intimately connected with his *Physics,* so that much of it is concerned with further conceptual analysis of ideas already introduced in the *Physics*—contrariety, nature, causality, form, potency, etc. But the core of the *Metaphysics* has to do with the ultimate causes of all reality. The immaterial and immovable prime mover, which Aristotle identifies with God, causes eternal circular motion (A-MET, XII, 7, 1072b, 10; 8, 1073a, 14ff.) of the spheres of the universe by his/its absolute attractiveness or "appetibility" (A-MET XII, 7, 1072a, 20ff.); everything in the world—presumably including the intermediate intelligent substances which vivify subordinate spheres—is moved by love and moves its subordinates by love (A-MET XII, 7, 1072a, 23–1072b, 6). But the prime mover himself/itself, whose actuality is described as "self-thinking thought" (A-MET XII, 7, 1072b, 15ff.), completely transcends the universe it actualizes; he/it does not seem to have any knowledge of things in the world, even indirectly, and does not exist in space in any sense.[3] In the sublunary sphere, living beings generate others, thus producing through the generation of individuals some reflection of divine eternal motion. In the production of nonliving things and artifacts, some preexisting actuality must be presupposed, activating the proximate potentialities; and actuality is prior in the world as a whole (A-MET IX, 8, 1050b, 6-1051a, 2). Beings in the world as a whole are graded according to lack of potentiality and predominance of actuality.

It is ironic that Aristotle starts off by criticizing Plato's idea of subsistent forms, since he himself ends up with a pure form or pure actuality: a God completely outside the world, who causes all reality—like Plato's idea of the Good—by being desired. But Aristotle, unlike Plato, claims to deduce the ultimate immovable cause and incorruptible co-causes of all reality scientifically, from a systematic examination of physical reality.

Aristotle's approach—based on the principles of matter and form, potency and act; and including a cosmological proof of the existence of God, and even intimations of the survival of the human soul after death[4]—was incorporated into medieval Arabian thought and Catholic Scholasticism. In the Middle Ages, debates raged in university *disputationes* about details of interpretation of Aristotelian principles; but the system itself prevailed.

As time passed, some of the schools of Scholastic thought hardened into dogma. This happened not only in Catholic Scholasticism, but also in the Protestant version, which peaked in Christian Wolff's amalgam of Spinoza's methodology and Leibniz's rationalism in a traditional Scholastic framework. Wolff carried the already formalistic Scholastic methodology to extremes, with dry deductions *in ordine geometrico;* and it was this eighteenth-century version of the "science of first principles" that Immanuel Kant was most familiar with.

B. Kant's Critique of Metaphysics

In Kant's estimation, the traditional interest in "first principles"—transmitted from Aristotle to successive generations of philosophers, and illustrated in modern philosophy in the systems of Gottfried Leibniz and Christian Wolff—demonstrates a lamentable ongoing confusion in metaphysics between the empirical and the a priori:

> When metaphysics was declared to be the science of the first principles of human knowledge, the intention was not to mark out a quite special kind of knowledge, but only a certain precedence in respect of generality, which was not sufficient to distinguish such knowledge from the empirical. . . . Does the concept of the extended belong to metaphysics? You answer, Yes. Then, that of body too? Yes. And that of fluid body? You now become perplexed; for at this rate everything will belong to metaphysics. It is evident, therefore, that the mere degree of subordination (of the particular under the general) cannot determine the limits of a science (K-CPR, A843=B871ff).

Kant thought that this confusion about metaphysical boundaries was a serious tactical mistake, which led inevitably to an overextension of metaphysics, as it developed its hierarchies of existence shading off into empirical instantiations. In place of this counterproductive quest, Kant proposed a new, reformed metaphysics concerned with the "principles of pure reason." This new system of metaphysics, or "pure philosophy," begins with his *Critique of Pure Reason* as its first part (K-CPR, A841=B869). Here, and in Kant's "analytic" reformulation of the *Critique of Pure Reason, A Prolegomena to any Future Metaphysics,* Kant investigated the mechanisms and requirements of a priori synthetic judgments, in which a non-empirical expansion of concepts takes place, to determine the limits of what can possibly be known. Kant believed that, while mathematics and theoretical physics had made great progress by applying such judgments, traditional metaphysics had typically merely been making valid but uninteresting analytical (nonexpansive, purely definitional) judgments, and invalid, speculative, syntheses which transcended not only experience but all possible experience. Examples of such unwarranted extensions into the unknowable included proofs of the immortality of the soul, the existence of God, and the finitude of the world. His own mission, as he saw it, was to draw some limits beyond which future metaphysics could not and would not pass. His *Critique of Pure Reason* was a propadeutic for the attainment of this goal.

A major contribution of this *Critique,* in Kant's estimation, would be to destroy all the diseased branches of the old metaphysics, leaving only the roots (K-CPR, B24). Kant's ultimate objective, however, is positive rather than negative; it is nothing less than to build up a "system" of pure reason regarding nature and freedom, resulting in a metaphysics of nature and a metaphysics of morals (K-CPR, A11). From the surviving "roots" of metaphysics, Kant expected a new and viable system to blossom, extending itself judiciously and modestly, using strictly a priori synthetic procedures (K-CPR, B23), to the domains of morals and nature (K-CPR, A841=B869ff.).

With regard to morals, this project was carried out first in a rather straightforward way in Kant's *Fundamental Principles of the Metaphysic of Morals* (1785). Moral judgment in the paradigmatic sense, the "categorical imperative," the attributes and ramifications of which are examined in this treatise, is defined at the outset as "an *a priori* synthetical practical proposition."[5] According to Kant, the three forms of the categorical imperative are based on the three initial "categories of quantity" already deduced in his *Critique of Pure Reason:* unity, plurality, and totality (K-FPMM, 53). Thus Kant's moral philosophy is best understood as a practical extension of categorial forms, unearthed in the *Critique of Pure Reason,* to the processes of moral judgment.

But the theoretical aspect of Kant's metaphysical project turned out to be much more challenging and problematic; it occupied his attention to the end of his life. Some progress in this project had been made in the *Critique of Pure Reason* itself. As Körner observes,

> The Transcendental Analytic gives . . . at least a partial answer to Kant's . . . question about the possibility of scientific metaphysics. Since metaphysical principles, as he conceives them, are all of the synthetic *a priori* judgements which are not mathematical, the *a priori* principles of natural science together with their logical consequences belong at the same time to a scientific metaphysics, the 'metaphysic of nature', as Kant calls it.[6]

Two good examples of what Kant would consider progress in scientific metaphysics can be found in the Analogies of Experience. In the First Analogy of Experience (K-CPR, A182=B224ff), he claims to offer philosophical justification for the traditional metaphysical idea of the permanence of substance; in the Second Analogy of Experience (K-CPR, A189=B232ff), he provides the a priori synthetic grounding for the "principle of causality," which had been attacked by David Hume.

But problems of ambiguity are connected with the metaphysical endeavors of the *Critique of Pure Reason,* as Kemp Smith points out. Scientific or "immanent" metaphysics is distinguished at the outset of the *Critique* from transcendent metaphysics, which goes beyond the bounds of possible experience to indulge in unverifiable speculations; and in general the positive content of immanent metaphysics is expounded in the Transcendental Analytic of the *Critique.* But in many parts of the *Critique,* Kant uses the term "metaphysics" and fails to distinguish whether he is referring to the immanent or transcendent type.[7] Even where it is clear that the references are to immanent metaphysics, there is a frequent confusion between two very different questions: 1) How are the existing a priori synthetic judgments to be explained? And 2) How can we discover and prove all the fundamental a priori synthetic judgments (KS 52)? Immanent metaphysics is also compromised by intermittent mention of a thing-in-itself (or transcendental object), which has no place in the *Critique,* compromises Kant's position that the thing-in-itself is just a projection of one's own subjectivity, and ascribes categories like substance and cause to the thing-in-itself, so that they lose their a priori applicability to phenomena (KS 204-218). And there is a further confusion between immanent metaphysics and natural science, aggravated by the fact that clear distinctions between universal and relative natural science are seldom made (KS 69-70).

The *Critique of Pure Reason* was just the "propadeutic" to Kant's projected system (K-CPR, A841=B869). The next step in Kant's ambitious metaphysical enterprise would involve the extension of the theories in the *Critique* about the categories, the schemata, and the transcendental principles of "nature in general" to *corporeal* nature. This would be a nonempirical, purely philosophical undertaking. By carefully developing the implications of the pure categories of the understanding, Kant insisted, philosophy can and will finally be delivered from the wasteful occupations of previous metaphysics, which had continually produced opinionated, unverifiable (and not even falsifiable) statements about the finitude or infinitude of the world, the ultimate nature of matter, the existence and attributes of God, the nature of angels, the essence of the soul and proofs of its immortality, and so on.

Kant's metaphysics of nature is extensively developed in the *Metaphysical Principles of Natural Science* (1786), in which all the categories deduced in his *Critique of Pure Reason* are systematically applied to various levels of movement in physical objects, as perceived in outer intuition. Studiously avoiding all speculative attempts to treat issues transcending possible experience, Kant endeavors to remain in this treatise on the cautious, conservative level of the sorts of "immanent" judgments philosophers can make about the physical world. But as Förster points out, Kant seems to waver as to how the treatise should be categorized: initially, he seemed to consider the *Metaphysical Principles of Natural Science* a contribution to "transcendental philosophy," even though it deals with an empirical concept of matter; but later, he seems to consider it a metaphysical work that provided a transition to transcendental philosophy. He also wavers in his definitions of transcendental philosophy and metaphysics. Finally, shortly before his death, he distinguished metaphysics, as the science which analyzes "given concepts," from transcendental philosophy, which contains the principles of synthetic judgments a priori and their possibility.[8]

Kant's constant frustrating efforts to carry his metaphysical project further can be seen in his voluminous posthumously published writings. He was still trying to extend his theory of the transcendental unity of apperception and the categories to the a priori synthetic cognition of, for example, the ego's self-positing, the existence of aether, the types of physical energy, and secondary qualities; and he filled page after page with sometimes seemingly unconnected thoughts, giving rise among his critics to allegations of senility. But Kemp Smith points out that many of these posthumous writings were penned at the same time as other later and well-organized published works; and that Kant characteristically did his rough work in this manner, jotting down thoughts from every conceivable angle before selectively reorganizing them for publication (KS, 609). So these unpublished and unpublishable endeavors may conceivably be viewed as a struggle to arrive at a state of clarity with regard to the position and functions of metaphysics.

Kant's unsuccessful efforts to complete a new system of metaphysics do raise questions about the viability of his project as a whole, and specifically about the idea of extending the categories of his *Critique of Pure Reason* as a kind of exhaustive set of the modes of understanding to all possible a priori nonempirical and nonmathematical cognitions. Schopenhauer, with his customary acerbity, discusses the widespread skepticism about Kant's metaphysical project:

> [The table of categories] is not only the foundation of the whole Kantian philosophy, and the type according to which its symmetry is carried through everywhere, . . . but it has also really become the Procrustean bed on to which Kant forces every possible consideration by means of a violence . . . In every inquiry conducted by Kant, every quantity in time and space, and every possible quality of things, physical, moral, and so on, is brought under those category-titles, although between these things and those titles of the forms of judging and thinking there is not the least thing in common, except the accidental and arbitrary nomenclature . . . What in the world has the quantity of judgments to do with the fact that every perception has an extensive magnitude? What has the quality of judgments to do with the fact that every sensation has a degree?[9]

On the one hand, the idea of constructing a new a priori synthetic metaphysics held promise of being the finest hour of human cognition, bringing the rationalistic tendencies of the eighteenth century to their natural culmination. Some would say that Kant attained some success in developing a metaphysics of morals; but most will agree that Kant failed to bring the ambitious project of an immanent, speculative metaphysics of nature very far beyond the planning stage.

C. Hegel versus Kant on Categories

Criticism of Kant's table of categories was one of the few things on which Schopenhauer and Hegel found themselves in agreement. In the *Phenomenology of Spirit,* Hegel focuses in particular on the arbitrary way in which Kant "deduces" the twelve categories from the various types of judgment:

To scare up the multiplicity of categories again [after Aristotle] in any old manner—for example, out of the types of judgment—as a "find," and to let oneself be satisfied with this state of affairs, should be regarded as a disgrace to [philosophical] Science. Where is the Understanding supposed to demonstrate any necessity if it does not already possess this power of demonstration within that pure necessity which is Understanding itself? (PSK, §235)

To Hegel, the issue was clear: if the Understanding has to go outside itself to derive metaphysical categories from a list of the types of judgment drawn up by Aristotle, any claim of "necessity" for the resultant categories is purely gratuitous. If the Understanding does not have any immanent method for substantiating the necessity of its categories, it should give up the attempt altogether. Thus a completely different approach to deriving categories is required.

One can speak in a general way of the "categories" in Hegel's Logic and *Realphilosophie;* but in a strict sense, for Hegel there is only one category: the category of the "identity in distinction" of being and thought, ego and reality, subject and object. Convinced that Kant was misguided in trying to deduce categories from the various types of logical judgment, Hegel set out in his *Phenomenology of Spirit* to provide an immanent, experiential approach to unearthing *the* paradigmatic category. The phenomenological process in that work involved a systematic dialectical oscillation between consciousness and its object, between conscious certainty and objective truth—a dialectic which (like a pendulum) brought the two extremes closer and closer together as the oscillation became more intense. Finally, there developed a moment in the *Phenomenology* when there was no further discernible separation between the opposites, and a point of highest activation was reached where the extremes were transparently transformed into each other in a state Hegel called *die Sache selbst.*

Die Sache selbst is Hegel's response to Kant's "thing in itself." Literally, it means "the real thing" or, in this context, "the really real." What Hegel is getting at is that the pseudodichotomy between the ego and a conjectured "thing in itself" has at this point disappeared; and that, if the analysis has been successful, the reader should at this point actually experience the new category:

> The [originally in earlier sections of the *Phenomenology*] formal *Sache selbst* has now come to its completion. . . . The Category is in-itself, as the universal of pure consciousness; and it is also for-itself, since the self of con-

sciousness is likewise its Moment. It is absolute Being, since the universality we have just referred to is the simple identity-to-self of Being. . . . It is the absolute "thing" [*Sache*] which is no longer affected by the opposition between certainty and the truth corresponding to it, or the opposition between the universal and the particular or an end-in-view and the reality of this end-in-view; rather, the existence of this "thing" is reality *and* the accomplishment of self-consciousness. . . . It is accounted "the absolute," because self-consciousness cannot, and does not intend to, proceed beyond this object; self-consciousness cannot go further, since the object in this case is all Being and all [spiritual] power; it does not will to go further, since the object is the self or the will of the self (PS, 277).

The Category Hegel is referring to here, like Heidegger's *Dasein,* might be called "he" or "she" as well as "it," for it is a type of consciousness as well as a category. It is the Idealist who has arrived at an insight of the identity-in-distinction of thought and being and has superseded all abstract interpretations and applications of this identity, finally arriving at a concrete experience of this Category within self-consciousness itself. Rather than saying that individuality at this point arrives at an insight of the Category, it would be more accurate to say that he or she *is* the Category. In other words, a new type of subjective-objective Individuality has appeared in the world of experience, and correspondingly a new type of subjective-objective Category. The individual who rises to an insight of the identity of being and thought actually exists as this identity, as its source and perpetuator. At this stage, Reason does not possess the Category but *is* the Category. (Kierkegaard propounds a similar idea in his "aesthetic" works by insisting that one's "duty" is not anything outside oneself but *is* oneself.)

As the *Phenomenology* proceeds beyond the stage of *die Sache selbst,* Hegel (in the sixth chapter) goes into the ethical implications of the Category and then extends it further, into its metaphysical implications. First, the unity of thought and being is instantiated in an "ethical substance," in which citizens find, at least temporarily, a full reflection of their subjectivities in the polity which they create and perpetuate. Second, the Category takes the form of an "enlightened" type of consciousness which actively tries to reconcile all the oppositions in its environment. Third, it appears in "conscience," which tries to go beyond the Kantian dichotomy between duty and inclination by coordinating the two. Fourth (in the seventh chapter) it reappears in religion, which from time immemorial has been concerned with the ultimate reconciliation of subjectivity and objectivity. Finally, the most advanced, most sophisticated development, and the ultimate manifestation of the Category, is

"Absolute Knowledge" (in the eighth chapter): a stage in which the intellectual coordination of *being to thought* and *thought to being* has taken place in the context of modern philosophy itself. In this advanced stage of culture, the Category has come to its own. All further philosophical science, and any future metaphysics, must take this Category as its starting point or pivot.

D. The Necessity of Surpassing Kant

With regard to the nature and possibility of metaphysics, Hegel found himself in agreement with Kant on a number of issues. Hegel, like Kant, was critical of the "older" metaphysics, which, for example, made the soul into a thing with thinglike properties (E3, §389, Zusatz); he agreed with Kant that a metaphysics outside possible experience is untenable; he was also interested in the revitalization and reform of metaphysics; and he was, in particular, very impressed with Kant's tentative speculations in the *Critique of Judgment* and elsewhere concerning an "intellectual intuition" in which the distinction between subject and object, analytic and synthetic, would disappear. (On the other hand, he was disappointed that Kant did not carry this last insight to its logical conclusion or conclusions.)

However, Hegel disagreed emphatically with Kant about the nature of experience and knowledge. For example, on what *experiential* basis could Kant set out in his *Critique of Pure Reason* to analyze the "limits" of knowledge scientifically? How can we be sure that there are not limits to how much we can know about the "limits of knowledge" themselves (H1, §36)? For that matter, if we could know these limits of knowledge, we would also know what is beyond them, since "wherever there is a limit, there is an unlimited, just on the other side" (H1, §34). Hegel also ascribed the Kantian problem of the "thing in itself" to Kant's own excessive subjectivism, which ends up willy-nilly being burdened with a new thought-thing—the "thing in itself"—as a persistent reminder of the very objectivity he is trying to avoid (SL1, 45, 59). And Kant's emphasis on a distinction between analytic and synthetic is merely another offshoot of the same subjectivism, which is constantly looking for some kind of filling or content for concepts that would otherwise be empty. Kant did not realize that the only suitable content for metaphysics is *die Sache selbst,* which in the metaphysical context is called the "Idea," and which in the last analysis is just a more sophisticated version of Kant's own insight about "intellectual intuition."

Hegel's metaphysics, his response to the perceived deficiencies in Kant, is to be found in his logic. In Hegel's estimation, logic and metaphysics have always been implicitly akin to each other; and it was his purpose to make their point of conjunction explicit:

> Thought, as regards its content, is true only insofar as it is immersed in the thing. . . . Thoughts in this sense can be called "objective" thoughts, among which the forms considered directly in ordinary logic would be included, except for the fact that they are conventionally assumed to be forms of *conscious* thought. Aside from this assumption, *Logic* coincides with *Metaphysics*, the Science of things encapsulated in thought; thus encapsulated, they stand for the true nature of things. . . . In general we have to investigate the logical as a system of thought-determinations in which the disparity between "subjective" and "objective" (according to the usual connotation of these words) has vanished (E1, §23–24, and Zusatz).

The groundwork for this subjective-objective logic-metaphysics, as has been indicated above, was already established in Hegel's *Phenomenology* with the generation of *die Sache selbst* and the "Concept" or "Idea." In the Introduction to his *Science of Logic,* Hegel reminds his readers that this preparatory work has already been successfully accomplished; and he seems to expect them to have this preparatory reading behind them:

> In my *Phenomenology of Spirit* I have exhibited consciousness in its progressive movement from the initial immediate opposition between itself and its object all the way to Absolute Knowledge. This procession [of stages] transverses all the forms of the *relationship of consciousness to the object* and has as its result the *Concept of Science.* This Concept (leaving aside the fact that it reemerges within the Logic itself [i.e., in the "Logic of the Concept"]) thus needs no justification, since it has already been justified in the *Phenomenology;* and it could not be justified in any other fashion than precisely by the aforesaid generation through consciousness, all of whose configurations are distilled into this Concept as into their truth (SL1, 42).

Having done his "homework" in *Phenomenology,* and assuming that his readers are familiar with the earlier work, Hegel compares and contrasts his own approach to developing a logic-metaphysics with Kant's approach in the *Critique of Pure Reason.* He sees considerable merit in what Kant and his followers attempted but resolves to avoid the epistemological impasse that inevitably emerged because of Kant's enthusiasm for a pure "transcendental" vantage point:

I grant that the Critical philosophy had already transformed *Metaphysics* into *Logic;* but the Critical philosophy, and subsequent idealism, out of its dread of object-encounter, gave the logical determinations an essentially subjective connotation; because of this, these philosophies remained weighted down with what they were fleeing from—the object; and a thing-in-itself, or an infinite "stoking",[10] remained as a "beyond" standing over against them. . . . Since the interest of the Kantian philosophy was oriented towards the so-called "Transcendental" aspect of the thought-determinations, the treatment of these determinations ended up empty. What are the determinations in themselves, aside from their abstract, mutually equal relationship to the ego? What is their distinction over against, and their relationship to, one another? [For the Critical philosophers] these questions do not become objects for consideration. Thus the knowledge of the nature of these thought-determinations has not been furthered in the least by the Critical philosophy (SL1, 45, 60–61).

To show how his own metaphysics would go beyond Kantian metaphysics, Hegel provides an example from the "Antinomies of Pure Reason" in the "Transcendental Dialectic" of Kant's *Critique of Pure Reason.* To begin, Hegel concedes that Kant's analysis of the dialectical relationship between the concepts of finite and infinite space and time, etc., was important for progression beyond the "old" metaphysics:

> Kant's treatment of [four cosmological] antinomies was a very important result of the Critical philosophy, and deserves recognition, insofar as the actual unity of the determinations held rigidly apart by the Understanding is expressed. Thus, for example, in the first cosmological antinomy it is implied that space and time are not only to be considered as continuous, but also as discrete, while, in contrast, the old Metaphysic remains fixed in mere continuity and, correspondingly, the world is thought to be unlimited with respect to space and time. . . . The same sort of observation holds for the remaining antinomies: for example, [with regard to the third antinomy, freedom-necessity] what the Understanding apprehends as "freedom" and "necessity" are actually just ideal moments of the true freedom and the true necessity, and no truth attaches to their separated state (E1, §48, Zusatz).

But this analysis was nevertheless incomplete, since Kant did not take it to its logical conclusion or conclusions. Kant's *Critique of Pure Reason* got only to the point of highlighting antithetical relationships between certain selected paired determinations that had been considered fixed and out of context in the "old" metaphysics; and his later *Metaphysical Principles of Natural Science* was not able to make any further progress beyond this point (SL2, 539). Hegel plans to take up where Kant leaves off. Hegel's logic-metaphysics would proceed further, to establish the unities in difference among these and other traditional metaphysical determinations.

E. Hegel's Logic-Metaphysics

Hegel's metaphysical enterprise takes place primarily in what, in his *Science of Logic,* is called the "Objective Logic." This is the first volume, comprising the first two of the three sections of the *Science of Logic,* that is, the Doctrine of Being and the Doctrine of Essence:

> Objective Logic now takes the place of the former "metaphysics" as that which used to be the scientific superstructure over the world, supposed to have been constructed solely by *thought.* If we take into account the finalized form of development of this science, we find that objective logic first of all replaces "ontology," the part of metaphysics that is supposed to investigate *being* in general. . . . But next, Objective Logic includes the rest of metaphysics also, insofar as these other parts seek to grasp with pure thought-forms particular represented substrata—the soul, the world, God—and insofar as *thought-determinations* provided the *essential* focus in their treatment. But [Objective] Logic considers these forms independently of those substrata, those subjects of *representation,* and treats of their nature and significance in and for themselves (SL2, 61).

In other words, the defect of the "old" metaphysics was that it focused too intently on connecting thought-determinations or logical categories with specific, popularly represented, substrata, thus missing the dialectical interconnections of the categories; as a result, it lost the life and spirit which give meaning to the categories of the Understanding. By contrast, in the Objective Logic that replaces the former metaphysics, instead of—for example—discussing the personal identity or simplicity of the soul, Hegel will consider the relationships between identity and difference, simplicity and complexity; instead of speculating about the reality or the finitude or infinitude of the world, he will analyze the dialectical relationships between reality and appearance, finite and infinite; and rather than attempting to prove the existence of God as first cause, he will discuss the nature of existence and the absolute, and of the ideas of priority and causality.

Hegel's Objective Logic, as his contribution to "reformed meta-physics," is concerned, then, with presenting the major metaphysical categories in their living, organic interconnections. Thus we find that one category will lead to an opposite—not just any opposite, but its own specific opposite, and in such a way that the opposition is generated out of the initial category itself.

This happens differently in the two subsections of Objective Logic. In the first subsection, the Doctrine of Being, the relation of Being to Nothingness is at first only implicit; it becomes explicit only with the realization that Being is pure indeterminate thought about nothing in particular. Similarly, quantity is at first only implicit in quality; it becomes explicit only after the orientation of qualities to otherness and outsidedness becomes subject to thought. In the second subsection, the Doctrine of Essence, the pairs and polarities and oppositions are explicit from the start: positive and negative, identity and difference, thing and properties, inner and outer, etc., are all considered in terms of their specific interrelationships.

What, then, are we to say of the second volume of the *Science of Logic:* "Subjective Logic"? As was mentioned above,[11] Hösle finds the largely bipartite division of the *Science of Logic* inconsistent with Hegel's general procedure, which is intended to go from (1) objective and (2) subjective to (3) a synthesis of subjective and objective. Hösle sees indications in the Logic in the *Encyclopedia* that Hegel was trying to move away from the earlier division, by shifting some analyses of subjectivity from the third to the second subdivision. A partial response to Hösle may be that Hegel was intent on presenting the former metaphysics again in the context of his Logic, just as he presents Aristotelian syllogistic logic again in a new context in the Subjective Logic (in the second and third chapters). In other words, the first volume—the two subsections given the general title "Objective Logic"—comprises Hegel's reconstituted metaphysics. The second volume—the subsection entitled "Subjective Logic"—has to do primarily with the subjective-objective Idea; it still begins with the concept of subjectivity, and Hegel presumably meant it to mark a clear departure from metaphysics of any sort, to "Speculation." The transition to "Subjective Logic" is the transition to Hegel's idea of a System constructed around the Idea, and able to unify and transcend previous systems, including metaphysics.

F. Metaphysics after Kant and Hegel

Kant was partially successful in inhibiting the speculative instincts of metaphysicians. For instance, in today's texts on metaphysics, one finds anxious questions about the possibility of making a priori synthetic judgments in metaphysical investigations; and much discussion is devoted to what Kant designated the "analytical" functions of metaphysics. This is valid and unobjectionable, Kant would say, but it does little to expand the horizons of philosophical knowledge. It would include analysis of concepts of—or language about—causation, space, time, nothingness, "thinghood," consciousness, necessity, individuality, reality, unity, etc. Present-day work in continental Europe on hermeneutics and phenomenology seems also to remain on a level that Kant would call analytic, or premetaphysical, avoiding speculation about God, the world, or the soul. As mentioned above, though, much of Aristotle's metaphysics was also devoted to analysis of words and concepts.

However, in today's metaphysics there is also occasional speculation; metaphysicians now and again make new attempts to justify earlier proofs, and occasionally propose new proofs, of the existence of God, the immortality of the soul, or free will—subjects that are still presumed to be beyond the boundaries of our possible experience. So Kant was not completely successful.

A strange contemporary phenomenon—possibly due to the tremendous advances in the physical sciences—is that scientists often enter areas that were once the province of only the most ambitious speculative metaphysicians. Thus we find quantum physicists speculating about the existence of consciousness in microparticles; cosmologists developing theories about how the world was created and the possibility of multiple universes or dimensions of existence; evolutionists, like Teilhard de Chardin, offering new theories about the creation of the human soul and the existence and nature of an "omega" (God); psychologists, like Jung, presupposing the existence of a communal human unconscious; parapsychologists speculating about the existence and locus of departed souls; and so forth. Metaphysics as a specialized discipline in our contemporary world seems, in comparison, quite chastened and rather conservative.

Hegel, of course, issued no strictures against metaphysical speculation, and even considered speculation to be within the limits of possible human experience. But the speculation that Hegelianism has given rise to has been very untraditional; examples from both "left" and "right" Hegelianism include Ludwig Feuerbach's thesis that God is the result of projections of ultimate human potentialities, David Strauss's demythologized Christianity and concomitant pantheism, John McTaggart's rejection of the reality of space and time, and Francis Bradley's ultracommunitarianism. Unfortunately much of the metaphysical speculation inspired by Hegel seems to be incognizant of the central position of the subjective-objective Idea in Hegel's system; very few have tried to follow in Hegel's footsteps by recognizing this centrality, although there have been some attempts on the part of those conscious of subjective-objective problematics to create a revised dialectical logic-metaphysics.[12]

The procedures and presentation of Hegel's "Objective Logic" seem to be largely products of styles of thinking and writing in early-nineteenth-century German idealism. One would not expect such an exemplar to be closely imitated in our own time. But granted that the approach and style would have to change, it seems incontestable that any future metaphysics based on the Hegelian pattern would distinguish itself by giving explicit attention to polarities and subjective-objective dynamics, systematically organized. Traditional subjects could be treated—God, freedom, etc. But God would no longer be treated as purely transcendent, freedom would no longer be treated in abstract isolation from necessity, and so on. This, in any case, would be Hegel's, as contrasted with Kant's, prescription for a reformed, valid and viable future speculative metaphysics.

II. Philosophy and the Special Sciences

A. Hegel and the "Two Cultures"

C. P. Snow's widely discussed book *The Two Cultures and the Scientific Revolution* (1959) brought to the attention of the general public a long-exisiting rift between the humanities and the physical sciences, of which there already was, and still is, considerable awareness and acceptance. This rift seems especially evident in the relationship between philosophy and the sciences. Snow's skepticism about the possibility of meaningful communication between the "two cultures" made some traditionalists nostalgic for pre-Baconian times, when philosophy and the various sciences were intertwined, it seemed inseparably—before scientific method began its ascent to preeminence in the hierarchy of cognitive disciplines.

It would seem that Kant, not fully realizing the full impetus of the Enlightenment currents he was following, innocently thought that his critical onslaught on the excesses of speculative metaphysics would ultimately bring about a closer relationship between the empirical sciences and philosophy—philosophy providing a priori guidelines and "pure principles" which would give direction to empirical science and promote clear, systematic scientific theorizing. In our contemporary culture, very few philosophers have continued in Kant's footsteps; most opt for guidance or mentorship as the role of philosophy. Husserl and Whitehead wanted to carry on the Kantian tradition, but for the most part the rift has widened.

Hegel, as we saw, drew away from pure a priori Kantian metaphysics—which he saw as a timid, escapist retreat into dualism, based on profound miscalculations about the powers of speculative Reason. Reason, as the power to coordinate dialectical oppositions between subject and object, a priori and a posteriori, through the Idea, would also be capable of bridging the newly opening gap between philosophy and the empirical sciences. In particular, the sharp and artificial division of the empirical sciences (having to do with sense experience and observation) from philosophy (dealing with abstract universals) had to be overcome.

B. The Dependence of Philosophy on the "Special Sciences"

Hegel, in commenting on the relationship of philosophy to the empirical realm, and on the fact that philosophy in a sense requires something "immediate" to subject to a process of "mediation," makes a quaint but illuminating analogy to eating:

> If "mediation" is made into a condition [for philosophizing] and emphasized in a one-sided way, one could say (although this is not saying much), that philosophy is indebted to experience (the "*a posteriori*") for its initial emergence; it is a fact that thinking is essentially the negation of something immediately present. But in the same vein one is indebted to food, since without food we cannot eat; eating, in this context, is of course not represented as receiving the credit, since eating is just the consumption of something to which it itself is indebted. So also, in this sense, philosophical thinking does not get the credit [for its "mediation"] (E1, §12).

In the case of a philosophy of nature, however, the "immediacy" to which philosophy must (somewhat begrudgingly and belatedly) acknowledge indebtedness is not an immediacy of first-order sense objects or events or even sense data already modified by subjectivity; but rather the relative immediacy of concepts developed and coordinated in the special sciences:

> The material prepared out of experience by physics is taken by the philosophy of nature at the point to which physics has brought it, and reconstituted without any further reference to experience as the basis of verification (E2, §246, Zusatz).

What physics does is bring empirical material to the conceptual level, where it can be accessible to philosophy—which works entirely on the conceptual level:

> Not only is the object to be provided [by physics] according to its conceptual determinations in the process of philosophizing, but the empirical appearances corresponding to these determinations has also to be made known, and the fact that they do in fact correspond (E2, §246).

More precisely, physics

> is oriented towards the knowledge of the *universal* in nature, to bring out the intrinsic determinations of this universal—the forces, the laws, the genera—a content, furthermore, that has to be not just a mere aggregate, but must be apprehended as organized into orders and classes (E2, §246, Zusatz).

But the universals thus attained, although they represent a tremendous accomplishment of the human intellect, nevertheless contain two major deficiencies:

> (1) The universal of physics is abstract, i.e. merely formal; it does not contain its determination in itself, it does not pass over into particularity. And (2) the determinate content is for this very reason outside of the universal, and thus split up, fragmented, isolated, segregated, lacking any interconnections—in other words, merely finite (E2, §246, Zusatz).

And this is where philosophy becomes relevant. Physics *qua* physics has done as much as it can, in discovering and cataloguing the various abstract universals in natural phenomena. Philosophy must proceed further to show the relationship of the abstract to the concrete and the interconnections of concepts.

C. The Contributions of Philosophy to the "Special Sciences"

Before dealing with the special sciences, philosophy must first prepare itself by working diligently in the "shadowland" of pure logic:

> The system of logic is the realm of shadows, the world of simple essentialities, liberated from all sensory concretions. The study of the science

of logic, residing and laboring in this shadowland, constitutes consciousness's absolute cultivation and discipline. Consciousness operates in logic far from sense-intuitions and the goals of the senses, far from feelings and from the world of commonly believed notions. . . . But in this way thought rises to self-sufficiency and independence. It gains a facility with the abstract, a facility in progressing through concepts without sense substrates, and attains the unsuspected power of raising the various and sundry sciences and bodies of knowledge to rational form, grasping and preserving what is essential in them, stripping off their externalities, and, in this way, . . . filling up the studiously acquired abstract logical foundation with the content of all truth, giving it universal value (SL1, 55–56).

Philosophy as a general "science of sciences" (H1, §9) includes many empirical sciences in its purview. It stands at the boundaries of other sciences, as an "interested observer" of the universal laws and general categories they arrive at empirically, but then tries to go further in coordinating these abstract "givens" and showing their relationship to the Idea of Reason. Provided that their contingent, factual, "positive" findings have been set to one side, philosophy includes the fundamental rationales for empirical sciences like natural history, geography, medicine, and jurisprudence, and it can deal constructively with such sciences (H1, §10). But philosophy has a special affinity with physics; and a viable philosophy of nature depends in particular on the close coordination of physics and metaphysics:

> Physics must be brought within the parameters of philosophy, so that the universalized understanding which physics provides may be translated into the Concept. . . . The philosophy of nature distinguishes itself from physics on account of the metaphysical procedure it employs, for metaphysics is nothing but the range of universal thought-determinations, and is as it were the diamond-net into which we bring everything in order to make it intelligible (E2, §246, Zusatz).

The "diamond net"—the sifter—which metaphysics supplies is the concatenation of essential dialectical relationships analyzed in Hegel's Logic. Although these logical relationships are developed in the rarified atmosphere of the pure Concept, they have wide applicability in the *Realphilosophische* realms of Nature and Spirit:

> Everything around us can be treated as an exemplification of the dialectical. . . . [Dialectic] is substantiated as valid in all the various levels and forms of the natural and spiritual world (E1, §81).

In physics, a close approximation to dialectics has already been made by the physicists themselves, in the various theories of polarity with regard to electricity, magnetism, etc. (E2, §248, Zusatz). What still needs to be done, as philosophy sifts through physical theory with the metaphysical "diamond net" is to bring out the many unities-in-opposition that physicists have overlooked or taken for granted in their preoccupation with the empirical. Thus Hegel in his Philosophy of Nature goes a step beyond prevailing physical theories; he focuses, for example, on dialectical relationships between mathematical points and the tridimensionality of space, the interconnection of time and space, temporal succession and coexistence, matter in motion and at rest, and the multiple paradoxes of light in relationship to corporeal bodies (see above, page 54). As he proceeds from physics to the latter parts of the Philosophy of Nature and into the Philosophy of Spirit, Hegel concentrates on the interrelationship between chemistry and electricity, chemical reactions between acid and base, the biological relationship between sensibility and reactivity, the effect of geography on personality and national character, etc. Such dialectical interrelationships constitute, in Hegel's estimation, a special type of universality. This is the fully integrating, "self-fulfilling" universality, which in its universal scope incorporates differences within its "diamond identity" (E2, §246, Zusatz). Hegel's metaphysical "diamond net," therefore, is a very specialized sifting device which processes great amounts of empirical data in order to salvage a limited number of conceptually meaningful identities-in-difference.

D. Hegel's Scientific Gaffes and Insights

Hösle points out that Hegel had a thorough knowledge of the science of his day, and that commentators on the Philosophy of Nature have a hard time rising to Hegel's level of scientific and mathematical knowledge (Hösle 277). Hegel's "diamond net" sifted "universals" provided by Copernicus, Galileo, Newton, Kepler, Laplace, Linnaeus, Lavoisier, Lamarck, and many other scientists, as well as by Schelling and Goethe in their scientific studies.[13] But experimental science was then in a state of comparative infancy; and this situation, sometimes combined with overoptimism on Hegel's part about the possibility of applying purely logical concepts to empirical reality, led him into errors. Thus Hegel (in contrast to Schelling) comes out strongly against the theory of biological evolution (E2, §249), disparages Newton's theory of motion, gravitation, and planetary motion in the light of Kepler's theory (E2, §270 and

Zusatz), and even tries—in an extremely conjectural leap—to demonstrate that the priority of heat over sound in organisms causes birds in
the tropics to become more distinctive in their plumage and colors than
in their song (E2, 303)!

Hegel's serious analysis of the ancient theory of the four elements
(E2, §§281–85) may also seem quaintly archaic, though Hösle defends
it as relevant to modern physicists' division of matter into four states:
solid, gaseous, liquid, and plasma states (Hösle 282). Hegel's adoption
of Goethe's theory of color and his rejection of Newton's theory may
also seem strange. But Petry maintains that this theory is "not without
its merits," since it goes beyond physics to analyze the *experience* of color
(E2P, 57), and Wandschneider defends Hegel's support of the theory as
the choice of a philosophically interesting approach over a philosophically uninteresting approach:

> Hegel's polemic against Newton makes it clear that he had in mind a dif-
> ferent kind of physics, a speculative physics that, for example, in the case
> of Goethe's theory of color, extracted the natural phenomenon from the
> clutch of methodical abstraction and grasped it in its unabridged totality.
> When Hegel makes an attack on physics, this has to be placed in the
> overall context of his ideal of a *unity* of science and philosophy—a philo-
> sophical physics. Thinkers like Aristotle, Kepler, Leibniz and Goethe
> seem to approximate to this endeavor. But with Newton there is no
> metaphysical context in view. Kant had consummated the explicit break
> in philosophy between science and metaphysics; Hegel then tries to put
> this development into reverse.[14]

Wandschneider goes on to argue that the first parts of Hegel's Philosophy of Nature—on space, time, matter and motion—are far from outdated; and that Hegel was at the forefront of the transition from the
classical, mechanical Newtonian concept of relativity to the Einsteinian
theory which replaced it (Wandschneider, 218). Hegel's Philosophy of
Nature as a whole is also defended by Hösle, as an essential building
block in his system, wrongfully ignored, containing important insights,
and often ahead of its time (Hösle, 277–81). For example, Hegel criticizes Newton's conjecture that a speeding bullet would keep going forever, if it were given a sufficiently high initial speed (E2, §266); this,
says Hegel, would be to take inertia in complete and unrealistic abstraction from gravity. According to Hösle, Hegel was vindicated in this by
Einstein's general theory of relativity, which holds that there is no such
thing as a gravity-free space.

H. S. Harris sees Hegel's Philosophy of Nature as fundamentally flawed, but nevertheless setting the stage for a new post-Hegelian philosophy of nature. He reasons that "the advance of science in the thirty years after Hegel's death made Hegel's own *Philosophy of Nature* appear absurd; but now that the advance has become a conceptual revolution, the *need* for a philosophy of nature is once more apparent."[15] Harris's point is that our new modern consciousness of the evolution of scientific paradigms, as epitomized in Thomas Kuhn's study *The Structure of Scientific Revolutions* "prepares the way for a Hegelian renaissance" (Harris 1983, 96), since it makes explicit for contemporary scientific consciousness the sort of conceptual dialectic that characterizes Hegel's Philosophy of Nature. And Harris believes that a revitalization of *Naturphilosophie* will be the special contribution of Anglo-Saxon Hegelianism, since "the *dominant* aspect of English speaking thought" is "the tradition of scientific empiricism"—the tradition of "Bacon, the apostle of experimental method, and of the co-operative development of applied science and technology" (Harris 1983, 94). Possibly the main thing lacking for a realization of Harris's sanguine vision is the "cooperative" element; in particular, collaboration between neo-Hegelian philosophers of nature and empirical scientists, which would seem to be necessary for the fulfillment of this "prophecy," is not yet on the horizon.

E. Foreshadowings of Heisenberg, Gödel, and Popper

In his Philosophy of Nature and elsewhere, Hegel develops ideas which are noteworthy anticipations of three contemporary theories in mathematics, science, and the philosophy of science which have received much exposure: Karl Popper's "falsifiability criterion"; Kurt Gödel's "incompleteness theorem," also called the "completeness theorem"; and Werner Heisenberg's "indeterminacy principle," also called the "uncertainty principle." However, the parallels discussed below show not only prima facie resemblances to the twentieth-century formulations, but also, as one might expect, some significant differences in context, intent, or both.

Popper's Falsifiability Criterion: In his book *Conjectures and Refutations: The Growth of Scientific Knowledge,* Karl Popper reminisces about how he first came to formulate his falsifiability criterion, which he had expounded in his earlier book *The Logic of Scientific Discovery.* He had been struck by the fact that Marxists, Freudians, Adlerians, and others seem to be very glib about explaining everything in the light of their theories. In the eyes of a dedicated theorist, there seemed to be nothing too remote to be eluci-dated by the theory. Then he compared the presumed "confirmations" of such theories with the explanatory power of Einstein's theory of gravita-tion, which risked *refutation* by actually predicting an observable event: that light from a distant star would be bent by gravity as it passed the sun. This is a theory that could be falsified through observation of a sub-sequent eclipse. But it was confirmed, not falsified, by Eddington's observations during the eclipse of 1919. To Popper, this is the sort of confirmation that really has "teeth" in it, and serves to distinguish sci-ence from pseudoscience—and from metaphysics.

Popper puts it this way:

> It is easy to obtain confirmations, or verifications, for nearly every the-ory—if we look for confirmations. Confirmations should count only if they are the result of *risky predictions;* that is to say, if, unenlightened by the theory in question, we should have expected an event which was incompatible with the theory—an event which would have refuted the theory. . . . One can sum up all this by saying that *the criterion of the scien-tific status of a theory is its falsifiability, or refutability, or testability.*[16]

Popper's criterion has been hailed as a way to clearly demarcate reliable scientific approaches from something like astrology, psychoanalysis, or metaphysics, whose "explanations" are suspect insofar as they try to explain too much—or everything.

A Hegelian parallel to Poppers's falsifiability criterion is found in the Philosophy of Nature (§304), where Hegel criticizes a current physical theory about "heat-matter." He denies the validity of this theory, siding with the Anglo-American scientist Benjamin Rumford, who maintained that heat was not a thing or substance or "matter," but a form of motion. Then, Hegel adds some comments (Remark and Zusatz to §305) which amount to his own "falsifiability criterion." He discusses the faulty procedures which led to the assumption that there is a latent "heat-material" which causes the warming of bodies, but still (allegedly) remains, although merely latent and invisible, when—for example—a body of low specific gravity becomes cold.

> The presupposition [that there is some such "heat-material," *Wärmestoff*] serves in its fashion to make the self-subsistence of heat as something material to be *empirically* irrefutable—*precisely because the presupposition itself is in no way empirical.* . . . It will not be admitted that heat, as a material substance, passes away, since it is self-subsistent; it is said therefore to be

merely "latent" and still present. But how can something be present and yet not exist? That sort of thing is an empty thought-figment. . . . (E2, §305 and Remark; italics mine)

Thus Hegel challenges this peculiar theory of heat precisely because it is empirically unfalsifiable and even characterizes it as *bad metaphysics* for the same reason, observing that "[this] metaphysics of self-subsistence is *opposed* to the *experience* in question, and is presupposed *a priori*."

This latter remark, however, brings out an important difference between Hegel's perspective and Popper's. For Hegel, metaphysics (unlike astrology or psychoanalysis) is not a set of unfalsifiable theoretical explanations. Rather, rightly understood and practiced, it simply takes up where valid, scientifically respectable physics leaves off, giving final conceptual form to the viable theories of physics. Thus the metaphysics that Hegel visualizes as operative in the Philosophy of Nature is not an autonomous discipline in the humanities, independent from what is going on in science; it is intimately related to science and even depends on the empirical data that science makes available to the philosopher.

The paragraph in which the question of the "heat-material" comes up is a good example of this. Here, Hegel is commenting on prevailing theories about the conduction of heat relative to specific gravity. He starts with the theories which he takes to be empirically verifiable (i.e., falsifiable in principle) and indicates how they are relevant to the conceptual "diamond net" he is putting together, to show (a few paragraphs later) how the partial transcendence of heat in a body evolves into the greater individuality of fire and flame. He intends to proceed further, to the analysis of magnetism and electricity, which are among the most striking manifestations of the Concept in the world of physics (that is, ideas which fit most explicitly into the metaphysical "diamond-net"). But his starting point is the "universal" theories which have already found a consensus among physicists, and which have been adequately verified through a procedure falsifiable in principle.

Heisenberg's Indeterminacy Principle: It is significant that Werner Heisenberg's "indeterminacy principle" is also called the "uncertainty principle." This reflects the difference of opinion between Heisenberg and Niels Bohr as to whether quantum phenomena were unsusceptible to precise measurement because of inevitable limitations of measuring instruments (Heisenberg's early view) or were unmeasurable *in principle*

(Bohr's view). In other words, are the strange events which take place in the world of microphysics, and which seem to defy the laws of local causality, merely subjectively uncertain, owing to the nature of the instruments which record wave functions and interactions? Or are they objectively indeterminate, like hermaphrodites that cannot be precisely characterized as male or female, or temperatures that cannot be described as hot or cold?

Heisenberg brings out the subjective-objective problematic in the following passage from his book *Physics and Philosophy:*

> The probability function [in quantum mechanics] combines objective and subjective elements. It contains statements about possibilities or better tendencies ("potentia" in Aristotelian philosophy), and these statements are completely objective, they do not depend on any observer; and it contains statements about our knowledge of the system, which of course are subjective in so far as they may be different for different observers. . . . Natural science does not simply describe and explain nature; it is a part of the interplay between nature and ourselves; it describes nature as exposed to our method of questioning. This was a possibility of which Descartes could not have thought, but it makes the sharp separation between the world and the I [ego] impossible.[17]

The constantly recurring example from quantum physics which illustrates the intermingling of subjective and objective factors is the "indeterminacy" resulting from efforts to measure the position and momentum of a subatomic particle. The sophisticated instruments used to measure the speed or momentum of a particle will cause uncertainty about its position; in other words, the measurement of its position must remain indeterminate, as long as our instruments focus on its momentum. By the same token, when its position is measured, its momentum becomes indeterminate. This sort of situation calls for a reevaluation of the apparently unambiguous precision which had been associated with classical or Newtonian physics. As Heisenberg puts it:

> The words "position" and "velocity" of an electron . . . seemed perfectly well defined as to both their meaning and their possible connections, and in fact they were clearly defined concepts within the mathematical framework of Newtonian mechanics. But actually they were not well defined, as is seen from the relations of uncertainty. One may say that regarding their position in Newtonian mechanics they were well defined, but in their relation to nature they were not (Heisenberg 85).

The "nature" that Heisenberg has in mind is not some purely objective set of entities and relations. Since the macrocosm is not subject to utterly different laws than the microcosm, we must assume that the same interweaving of subjective *and* objective factors also prevailed in Newtonian physics, although the precise results of mathematical formulae gave the appearance of purely objective assessments of reality. It is only in the modern, post-Cartesian era that we have become cognizant of just how much subjective procedures and methodologies and conceptual expectations can influence so-called "objective" calculations.

Heisenberg also considers Kant's *Critique of Pure Reason*—with its thing-in-itself, its subjective forms of space and time, and its conceptual categories, somehow making scientific objectivity possible—to be a major statement of the Cartesian heritage. He concludes with a critique of the neat subjective-objective distinctions drawn by both Descartes and Kant, and a metaphysical statement about the all-pervasiveness of indeterminacy:

> Any concepts or words which have been formed in the past through the interplay between the world and ourselves are not really sharply defined with respect to their meaning; that is to say, we do not know exactly how far they will help us in finding our way in the world. We often know that they can be applied to a wide range of inner or outer experience, but we practically never know precisely the limits of their applicability. This is true even of the simplest and most general concepts like "existence" and "space and time." Therefore, it will never be possible by pure reason to arrive at some absolute truth (Heisenberg 92).

The appropriate interpretation of the *interplay* between the world and ourselves is also a major Hegelian theme. The first paragraphs of Hegel's Introduction to his *Phenomenology of Spirit* describe the sort of impasse a Kantian focusing on the subjective conditions for objective knowledge must find himself in. First of all, there is a presupposition that knowledge is an instrument for getting at truth; if only we fully understand the ins and outs of this instrument—so the argument goes—we should be confident of arriving at true objective knowledge. Who knows? Perhaps Kant himself, as he began to work out the arguments of his First Critique, had hopes of sharpening the cognitive instruments to such precise tolerances that they would be able to grasp the Absolute—if not directly, then possibly by cleverly subtracting from the final results whatever the "instrument" had contributed. But in Hegel's estimation, there is something wrong with the way this whole problematic is set up. What is wrong is the initial a priori assumption that there is some kind of inviolable distinction between cognition and the objective truth which it wishes to grasp. As Hegel observes:

> The chief presupposition (of this critical standpoint) is that the Absolute stands *on one side,* and cognition for-itself *on the other,* as something real, even though sundered from the Absolute; or even, as a corollary, that cognition which, being outside the Absolute (and also quite outside the truth) nevertheless somehow is true! (Here we have a supposition wherein what calls itself "fear of error" reveals itself rather as fear of truth) (PSK, §74).

Hegel had serious differences with Fichte and Schelling, but he shared with them the goal of overcoming the artificial and counterproductive split between subjectivity and objectivity. In the Logic in the *Encyclopedia,* Hegel, like Heisenberg, portrays this split as the major defect in the standpoint of the Kantian "Critical" philosophy:

> It is said that the in-itself of things is something completely different from that which we make them out to be. The standpoint of this dichotomization has become especially prominent through the critical philosophy—in direct opposition to the prior convictions of the whole world, which understood the agreement of thing and thought as something to be taken for granted (E1, §22, Remark).

In his *Lectures on the History of Modern Philosophy,* Hegel uses the legendary account of a "scholastic" from Greek antiquity to further ridicule the epistemological split between cognition and thing:

> In Schelling's philosophy the content or the truth has once more become the main thing, whereas in the Kantian and the other subsequent philosophies the concern most particularly expressed was that knowledge, cognition, or subjective cognition should be investigated. It appeared plausible [to Kant et al.] that we should first investigate cognitive knowing, the instrument, although there is an old story told of the σχολαστικός who would not enter the water until he had learned to swim (HP3BS, 263).

But, granted that the scholastic was silly for thinking he could learn to swim, as it were, a priori, how does he avoid drowning if he ventures into the water without knowing how to swim? And how is it possible to attain true knowledge, of the Absolute or whatever, without hopelessly confounding objective reality with our subjective conceptions?

Hegel's approach to this problem in the *Phenomenology* is somewhat similar to Heisenberg's. Heisenberg's "indeterminacy" results in a dialectic. For example, in taking measurements of an electron, the physicist who focuses on its precise position must give up precision as to its momentum; and when measuring its momentum, the physicist will necessarily be uncertain as to its position. But in oscillating between these two alternatives, the physicist attains a *dialectical* profile of the particle in question. So also, in Hegel's phenomenology of sense-certainty, consciousness may focus on the particular "here" or "now" at the expense of the universal, or on the universal at the expense of the particular; and in the phenomenology of Understanding, consciousness may focus on Newtonian force as an objective phenomenon at the expense of the laws governing force, or vice versa.

But here an important difference between Hegel's and Heisenberg's approaches becomes apparent. The difference is that in Hegel's *Phenomenology,* the experience of dialectic drives consciousness to look for a privileged type of knowledge in which this oscillation will no longer be necessary. As we have seen, this is Absolute Knowledge, the subjective-objective source of the "absolute" standpoint prevailing in Hegel's Philosophy of Nature and the rest of his system. One may conjecture that, if Hegel had at his disposal the data of quantum physics concerning the position and momentum of microparticles, he would strive in his Philosophy of Nature to go beyond the dialectic oscillation pointed out by Heisenberg to capture the subjective-objective dynamics leading to that oscillation.

Gödel's Incompleteness Theorem: Kurt Gödel's "incompleteness theorem" is concerned with systems, but specifically with the nature of a mathematical system. If one accepts the arguments of Russell and Whitehead's *Principia Mathematica,* Gödel's theorem may also be applied to a system of formal logic built up from theorems and rules of inference.

In its original formulation, the incompleteness theorem reads:

> For every ω-*consistent recursive class* κ *of* FORMULAS *there are recursive* CLASS SIGNS $r,$ *such that neither* v Gen r *nor* Neg (v Gen$r$) *belongs to* Flg κ (where v is the FREE VARIABLE of r).[18]

A mathematician who is able to symbolize this theorem and number the variables in Gödelian fashion will have the easiest access to it. However,

John Findlay, in an interesting article, tried to translate the theorem into (more or less) ordinary English propositions. Findlay's translation is as follows:

> 1. Let F = "We cannot prove the statement which is arrived at by substituting for the variable in the statement-form Y the name of the statement-form in question."
>
> 2. Let G = "We cannot prove the statement which is arrived at by substituting for the variable in the statement-form F the name of the statement-form in question." Then make the substitution called for in G by replacing the variable Y in F with the name of the statement-form in question, which is F itself.[19]

If Gödel's "proof" is examined carefully, it can be seen to be recursive and undecidable. The theorem is intended precisely to prove that it is outside the parameters of its own proof system. Insofar as it seems to be proving its own unprovability, it is sometimes described as the counterpart, in the theory of natural numbers, of the famous "liar paradox" which has driven countless logicians to distraction. It is called the "incompleteness" theorem (and sometimes, paradoxically, the "completeness" theorem), because it maintains that a thoroughly consistent system in the theory of natural numbers would have to be incomplete (and, correspondingly, that a thoroughly complete system would necessarily fall into inconsistency). Thus in developing such a system, the mathematician would have to choose between perfect consistency and perfect completeness. In a rigidly consistent system in which every part was tightly connected with every other, there would be at least one instance not covered; and if the system tried to expand sufficiently to cover this and other such instances, its consistency would suffer as a result. So a reasonably realistic mathematician or logician would have to give up any hope of constructing a final, perfectly "airtight" system.

After the publication of Gödel's theorem, disputes broke out over its philosophical significance. Rudolf Carnap saw it as support for his goal of producing an analytic theory of linguistic structures on a mathematical model, without metaphysical presuppositions. Ludwig Wittgenstein criticized it for latent Platonism, in its supposition of a realm just beyond what is comprehensible. Many philosophers since then have commented on the metamathematical and epistemological significance—or insignificance—of the theorem. But there has been little interest in considering its applicability to strictly *philosophical* systems—not because of any Gödelian rationale, but because the development of a philosophical system is generally considered outmoded or in principle impossible.

Hegel's intellectual milieu was of course much more optimistic about the possibility of producing a philosophical system; and in his treatise *Natural Law,* Hegel makes an observation about the choice between consistency and completeness in a such a system. If we make allowance for the difference in contexts, Hegel's statements seem to parallel closely the thrust of Gödel's theorem. He addresses the problems of a would-be philosophical synthesizer as follows:

> At first empirical science encounters scientific totality as a totality of the multiplex, or as completeness; but authentic formalism encounters the totality as consistency. The former [empirical science] can at will raise its experiences to universality, and, with the determinations it has excogitated, stretch consistency so far that other empirical content which contradicts the previous content, but still has a right to be thought, and to be formulated as a principle, no longer corroborates the consistency of the previous determinacy, but forces its abandonment. [On the other side,] formalism can stretch its consistency as far as the emptiness of its principle permits, or as far as a content which it smuggles in can tolerate; but in this way it is justified, on its part, in proudly eliminating from its "a-priority" and science, what stands in need of completeness, designating it pejoratively as the "empirical"; for it upholds its formal principles as the "a priori" and absolute, and claims that whatever it cannot master through these principles is non-absolute and accidental.[20]

Hegel makes this statement in the context of an analysis of two extremes which a theorist of natural law could fall into. On the one hand is the extreme of empiricism, appealing in Hobbesian fashion to a "state of nature," an initial social chaos out of which lawful existence supposedly evolved. On the other hand is the extreme of "transcendental idealism"—as propounded by Kant and unsuccessfully revised by Fichte—trying to absorb all empirical data into some abstract formal universal schema. And in Hegel's *Science of Logic* we find that this situation in the practical sciences is mirrored in the theoretical sphere by the equally necessary choice between two philosophical extremes: the extreme of an internally consistent synthetic system *in ordine geometrico,* as exemplified in Spinoza's *Ethics;* and the extreme of an empirically complete analytic compilation of data without any governing unifying principle, as exemplified in Locke's *Essay on Human Understanding* (E1, §§227; 229, Remark, 231; SL 195, 250f).

Hegel's solution—and this is where the great difference between Hegel's position and Gödel's becomes apparent—was to focus on the self-moving and self-regenerating Idea, which overcomes the distinction between subjective and objective, synthetic and analytic, idealistic and empirical, method and content. In Hegel's system the Idea, which is patterned after the restless search-for-rest of human self-consciousness itself, is at one and the same time the method, the road, the way, and the sole meaningful content. It produces empirical completeness in a certain well-defined area: the system of categories. But it also produces ideal consistency for a certain type of second-order experience: the experience of Reason, which overcomes the distinctions of the Understanding. The speculative Idea, in Hegel's formulation—and this is a comparison that has been often made—is the philosophical equivalent of the λóγος in John's Gospel—the Word which is there in the beginning, and through which all essentialities are formed before the fall from unity. Thus Hegel suggests a way out of the completeness-consistency dilemma, as applied to philosophical systems, unlike Gödel, who leaves mathematicians in a dialectical impasse. What is sometimes considered a disadvantage of philosophy may in this case constitute a peculiar advantage: that it is expected to justify its own principles, whereas other disciplines, including mathematics, may quite legitimately and without the least embarrassment accept their foundational principles from other areas. In other words, philosophy, unlike mathematics, is *expected* to prove its provability.

It is extremely doubtful that Hegel's ideas had any direct influence on the formulation of these contemporary notions of falsifiability, indeterminacy, or incompleteness. Popper is noted for his acerbic criticisms of Hegel's political philosophy and certainly does not credit Hegel for any of his own insights; Gödel, although he was interested in Hegel and sometimes jotted down passages from Hegel, Kant, Fichte and other favorite philosophers, does not seem to have been inspired by Hegel's critique of system building; and Heisenberg, although familiar at least through secondary sources with many philosophical works (discussed, for instance, in his *Physics and Philosophy*), shows no direct influence of Hegel's subject-object problematic. So I present the above positions merely as three very interesting parallels between Hegel's system and twentieth-century developments in mathematics and science. If the parallels are there, then we may conclude further that these developments were anticipated in philosophy by Hegel.

III. Philosophical Anthropology

A. The Genealogy of Philosophical Anthropology

One can find certain lineaments of philosophical anthropology in the works of Rousseau (1712–1778) and Montesquieu (1689–1775); some would want to trace its origins back even further, to Pascal (1623–1662), Montaigne (1553–1592), or others. The rationale for attributing the origins of philosophical anthropology to any of these authors is that they all have in common a primary interest in asking new questions about human nature or proposing new approaches to answering old questions.

But philosophical anthropology as a distinct discipline is possibly first represented by Kant's *Anthropology from a Pragmatic Point of View* of 1798, which was the culmination of university lectures on anthropology that Kant had been delivering for many years. Kant's *Anthropology* was published toward the end of his life, and after the publication of his famous three *Critiques:* of pure reason, practical reason, and judgment. In *Anthropology,* Kant discusses many topics which today we might loosely categorize as psychological, anthropological, physiological, or possibly pseudoscientific—e.g., the external and internal senses, dreaming, talent, temperament, character, racial and national characteristics, and gender differences. To someone who is familiar with Kant's three *Critiques, Anthropology*—with its emphasis on what is observable in ordinary human experience—stands in sharp contrast to their strict, unwavering emphasis on the spiritual-intellectual aspects of humanity. It is almost as if Kant is trying to counterbalance the abstruseness of these earlier works by attending to various human traits or aspects which it might be "pragmatically" useful to know about. One of the contributions of *Anthropology* was to bring to the public certain findings in the empirical sciences, including data being received from new explorations in the non-European world, which could conceivably be of philosophical interest. The *Anthropology* was clearly meant to be a popular work, somewhat comparable to the numerous works of "pop psychology" published in our own day.

In the early nineteenth century, philosophical anthropology seemed to many—including commentators on Kant and critics of Kant—to offer a way of overcoming the Cartesian dualism which Kant himself had fallen prey to, by concentrating on the *embodied* psyche and the various natural and cultural influences affecting it. Numerous books were published on human temperament and physiognomy, gender differences, embodiment, psychosomatic medicine, etc.,[21] and Hegel read in this field with great interest. But a general characteristic of such works, as also of Kant's anthropology, was their unsystematic intermingling of physiological, psychological, anthropological and geographical considerations (E3, §444). Hegel saw his own contribution to this burgeoning field as making it more systematic and demonstrating its relationship to the dialectical-speculative Concept.

In the twentieth century, the term "philosophical anthropology" has generally connoted trends in existentialism, Phenomenology, and *Lebensphilosophie* and works by practitioners such as Max Scheler, Martin Heidegger, Ernst Cassirer, and Michel Foucault. What they have in common with the "classical" philosophical anthropology of the early nineteenth century is their interest in overcoming dualism—they focus on the human element even in purportedly "objective" types of knowledge—and an attempt to coordinate the findings of diverse sciences which contribute to an understanding of humanity. They differ from the "classical" anthropologists, however, in their opposition to mechanical, Newtonian concepts of science and technology; and they certainly differ from Hegel in their concepts of system or systematicity, and in their looser association with the "givens" of science—an association ranging from an ongoing dialogue with science to systematic challenges to science or technology.

B. The Place of Anthropology in Hegel's System

As I mentioned in Chapter 3 (page 28), Hegel portrays Nature as the Idea of Spirit in a condition of otherness. But since the Idea in its totality is still implicit in Nature, the natural world is replete with various approximations to Spirit, and the teleological stages of these approximations are charted by Hegel in his Philosophy of Nature. The highest approximations have to do with the emergence of life; and the further development of life supplies, as one might expect, the transition from the Philosophy of Nature to the Philosophy of Spirit:

> Philosophy in a certain sense needs only to stand by and observe how Nature itself supersedes its externality, reclaims its self-externalization at the center of the Idea (or better, lets this center emerge in the realm of externality); Nature liberates the Concept hidden within it from the shell of externality, and in this way transcends external necessity. This transition from necessity to freedom is not an easy one, but a progression

through many stages, the explication of which is the contribution of the Philosophy of Nature (E3, §382, Zusatz).

Anthropology takes up where Philosophy of Nature leaves off. As the initial stage of Subjective Spirit, it is the state in which Spirit is heavily intermingled with matter, so that at first only the bare outlines of Spirit can be discerned. The movement toward higher levels takes on the appearance of a primal struggle of Spirit to throw off its material constraints and rise above nature:

[As natural life attains to the state of feeling,] Spirit, existing in-itself and imprisoned in Nature, arrives at the vestibule of its existence-for-self, and thus its freedom. By means of this existence-for-self, even while still weighed down with the form of particularity and externality, and consequently with unfreedom, Nature is driven forth beyond itself to Spirit as such, in other words, to Spirit which exists for-itself through thought in the form of universality and is really free (E3, §382, Zusatz).

The quest of Subjective Spirit to actualize its highest potential proceeds teleologically from the earliest states, where Spirit is still deeply immersed in Nature and natural life, to the emergence of consciousness ("Phenomenology") and theoretical and practical reason ("Psychology"). This movement leads finally to the emergence of the ego, victorious over Nature, excluded from involvement with nature. This is the culmination of Subjective Spirit. Hegel uses metaphorical language to describe the outcome: the shame which Adam and Eve felt about their nakedness (Genesis 3:7–13) was just embarrassment about being part of nature; and with the emergence of ego, this embarrassment no longer overwhelms humans (E1, §24, Zusatz).

Hegel's treatment of philosophical anthropology, like his Philosophy of Nature, is intermediate between metaphysics and empiricism (E3P, 103). In the Philosophy of Nature he accepted prevailing "universal" theories in the physical sciences and tried to develop their philosophically interesting connections and implications. Similarly, his Philosophical Anthropology has as its starting point a broad acquaintance with theories and methods in psychology, and what we would now call parapsychology and anthropology and ethnology—Mesmer on hypnotism, Blumenbach on race, Pinel on insanity, and many other sources.[22] But the so-called "soft" sciences, in Hegel's time and now, fall short of the unanimity regarding acceptable theories that characterize the "hard" sciences (whose traditional paradigm is physics). Thus Hegel's philosophical anthropology was conditioned not only by the inchoate nature of the empirical sciences he was conversant with, but also by the continually oscillating flux of theories trying to deal with the complexities of human nature. As we examine some of the major positions in Hegel's Philosophical Anthropology, we may ask ourselves whether, in the current stage of development of psychology and anthropology, an updated attempt to organize and coordinate findings systematically and philosophically might not still be worthwhile.

C. Perennial Topics from a Hegelian Perspective

Human Evolution: As mentioned above (page 88), Hegel disagreed with Schelling about the possibility of physical evolution. Hegel's objections had to do primarily with the notion of a *physical* evolution of *species*. It is obvious that there is a gradation of stages in nature in Hegel's philosophy—from inorganic to organic to intellectual and spiritual. But these stages, Hegel maintains (E2, §249), are not to be associated with any *natural* development of one stage out of the other. To talk about a natural, physical progression of stages is tantamount to buying into materialism (E3, §389), which is a noble but misdirected attempt to close the gap between spirit and matter by tracing the development of spirit *per impossibile* out of matter. Such attempts do away with teleology, which is the spiritual side of evolution, as seen from the vantage point of the Concept (E2, §249). The theory of physical evolution, like the classical theory of emanation, is faced with the twofold task of extrapolating the evolution of individuals, which does take place, into a fictional evolution through time of the species, and of doing this without any concrete goal in view for the whole process:

> It is completely useless to present the species as evolving one after the other in time; such temporal differentiation is of no interest whatsoever for philosophy. . . . The process of evolution that [allegedly] begins with what is inchoate and formless maintains that initially there existed moisture and aqueous forms, then plants, polyps, mollusks, and fish came forth, then land animals; and from the animals finally humans arose. This gradual metamorphosis is dubbed "explanation" and "conceptualization," and this way of looking at things has gained ground in the Philosophy of Nature. But such quantitative differences, while they are easy to understand, actually explain nothing at all (E2, §249, Zusatz).

Although today the theory of evolution of the species is almost universally accepted, there are a minority of evolutionists who reject Darwinian "natural selection" or are looking for teleological or quasi teleological explanations, especially in view of the astronomical improbability of the evolution of intelligence from mere "natural selection."[23] It is probable that if Hegel were cognizant of contemporary "natural selection" arguments, he would dismiss them as "explaining nothing" but would also, in view of the empirical data, side with those who opt for a teleological interpretation of the evolutionary ascent toward humanity.

Race and Ethnicity: Europeans in the seventeenth and eighteenth centuries had been under the strain of trying to make sense out of the vast amounts of data coming from newly explored and newly colonized lands. Montesquieu in his *The Spirit of the Laws* and Voltaire in his *Philosophical Dictionary* theorized about causal connections between geography and climate, on the one hand, and the temperament and political orientations of peoples, on the other. Kant in his *Observations of the Feeling of the Beautiful and the Sublime* (which preceded his *Critiques*) offered a rather elaborate categorization of the various nationalities and races and the sexes, in terms of their orientation toward, and manifestation of, aesthetic qualities. Hegel's typology is of a piece with such endeavors, but it differs in his attempt to clarify the development of race and ethnicity in terms of the teleological evolution of the Concept or Idea.

The Idea of Nature had passed over, at the outset of Subjective Spirit, into a state of immediacy in which Spirit was just beginning to emerge in Nature and work its way upward toward consciousness and self-consciousness. In these preconscious stages, considered not as temporally prior, but as necessary conditions for all higher developments, incarnate Spirit divides itself up into the various races and ethnic-national groups.

Montesquieu was the first philosopher to speak of the "spirit of the nations" in a generic sense, characterizing an entire people as sharing one general spirit. It is possible that Montesquieu meant this in some literal, nonmetaphorical sense. In any case, Hegel's treatment of the development of race and ethnicity may be understood as an attempt to supply the conceptual underpinning for this idea—demonstrating how Spirit as a wholesale phenomenon has manifested itself worldwide in the various instantiations of *Volksgeist*.

As Hegel tries to elaborate this development in concrete detail, however, the results are replete with stereotypes. The natural soul (after initial development) differentiates itself into races (E3, §393, Zusatz):

Africans exemplify placid immediacy, Asians restless mobility, and Europeans self-movement—self-development. The races which were removed from the sea by circumstance (e.g., Africans) or by artificial moral restrictions (e.g., the people of India) seemed to have been slowest in reaching for freedom (E3, §394, Zusatz). The sections of Africa and Asia next to the Mediterranean are Caucasian-European in Spirit. The Europeans themselves best exemplify the principle of subjectivity. Italians are noted for immediate individuality; Spaniards are noted for individuality recognizing the universal (e.g., in "honor"); the French are notable for a synthesis of emotion and reason; the English excel in a kind of "intellectual intuition" which approaches the rational in the form of individuality. The Germans, finally, are oriented toward comprehending the inner rational nature of things, although they sometimes carry this tendency to formalistic extremes.

Hegel thus himself carries the then-prevalent Eurocentrism and Teutonicity to a formalistic extreme. Examples of these categorizations are also found elsewhere in Hegel's work; for instance, in his Philosophy of History he portrays the "immediate individuality" of the Italians as the cause of their perpetual tendency to disunity.[24] His classifications are useful historically, however, insofar as they sum up attitudes in European culture and also widely held scientific views of the time.

Temperament: Kant, in his *Anthropology from a Pragmatic Point of View*, discussed the traditional four-temperament theory of Hippocrates and Galen in some detail. During the nineteenth century, physiologists and psychologists searched for some physical basis for these temperaments—possibly hormonal or neurological characteristics—to replace the outmoded Hippocratean theory of bodily "humours." When these efforts proved unsuccessful, psychologists began to look for strictly psychological factors that could be verified independently of physiological or neurological conditions. Wilhelm Wundt (1832–1920) developed a typology based on Kant's four-temperament theory, but departing from Kant in that the four types which Kant thought to be unmixed and irreducible are reconstructed as two intersecting orthogonal dimensions (see Figure 10). This reconstruction has been influential in contemporary theories of differential psychology, the emotional-nonemotional dimension being renamed in terms of "stability" or "ego-strength" and the changeable-unchangeable dimension evolving into a nomenclature of "extroversion" and "introversion."

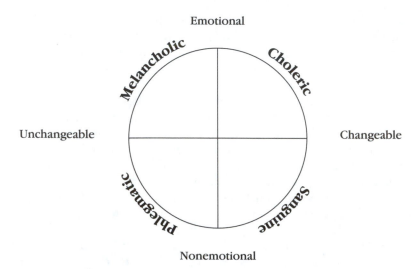

Figure 10. Wundt's typology of temperament.

Hegel indicates (E3, §395, Zusatz) that he is following Kant in differentiating the temperaments on the basis of whether there is a primary orientation to changeability (the sanguine and choleric temperaments), to single objects (phlegmatic) or to single-minded apathy (melancholic). This categorization runs parallel to contemporary theories, which reclassify the sanguine and choleric as "changeable-extroverted" and the phlegmatic and melancholic as "unchangeable-introverted," often with intersecting dimensions of emotional intensity. Hegel would very likely agree with Sheldon's definition of temperament as "the level of personality just above physiological function and below acquired attitudes and beliefs; . . . the level where basic patterns of motivation manifest themselves."[25] For in Hegel's system, temperamental orientation is the initial manifestation of the drive of embodied Spirit to go beyond generic racial or ethnic characteristics to individualization; but it is still preconscious and instinctive.

Developmental Psychology: Our contemporary branch of psychology known as "developmental psychology" is of relatively recent origin. Major twentieth-century figures in the discipline include Jean Piaget (1896–1980), Erik Erikson (1902–1994) and Arnold Gesell (1880–1961). Their pioneering work in the study of child and adolescent development paved the way for more recent psychological studies of mature development by Daniel Levinson, Gail Sheehy, and others. Most of these psychologists have used empirical (observational and experimental) approaches, ending up with theories about "stages" through which the normal person will pass in his or her psychological development. There are some notable correspondences between these theories and Hegel's analysis. Although Hegel's approach differs in its explicit teleological emphasis on development toward rationality, freedom, and intersubjectivity, it seems that developmental psychologists, on purely empirical grounds often, end up implicitly with a similar teleology.

Hegel (E3, §396, Zusatz) considers the totality of human existence, from fetal life to old age, as a movement out of exclusively corporeal conditioning to the expression of Spirit. The diversification of the human soul passes temporally through a series of stages. Prenatal existence is a human recapitulation of vegetative existence; infancy recapitulates animal existence, with the initial development of sensation and perception; toddlerhood marks the development of an ego-sense and language, and thus the entry into human existence in the strict sense. In childhood, the faculties are further developed through play, preparing the child for education. Moral education for the child consists in learning, through obedience, to control inclinations, and eventually identifying with concrete, personal ideals. In puberty and adolescence the ideals become abstract, sometimes pitting the adolescent against the world and the things it stands for. In adulthood, finally, if the development proceeds aright, a reconciliation with the world will be attained, and the salvageable essence of one's young ideals will be attained, possibly with some compromises or limitations, through work. In old age, we may often expect a loss of interest in the present, and a return to the immediacy of childhood and infancy.

Someone who is familiar with developmental psychology will notice similarities with current notions about which there is some consensus: the transition from indeterminate sensations to perception and ego-awareness in the first year, the "age of obstinacy" in toddlerhood, the "negative stage" of adolescence, the idealism or "dreams" of young adulthood, the "midlife crisis," etc.

Sensation and Feeling: Sensation in Hegel's philosophical anthropology is a state in which the soul is still immersed in matter but also beginning a movement toward Spirit. In the earliest version of the *Encyclopedia,* it is a final manifestation of the "natural determinacy of the soul," conceptually amalgamated with feeling (H3, §318), and leads eventually into a state of psychic antithesis (H3, §319). In the latest version it is considered the final subdivision of the section on the "physical soul" (E3, §401); also, a sharper distinction is made between sensation and feeling, and a more gradual transition to antithetical states (like insanity) is made in subsequent sections on the "feeling soul" (E3, §§403ff).

Hegel's systematic analysis of sensation and feeling shows some interesting parallels to the no less systematic treatment by Thomas Aquinas in his *Summa theologiae*. In his article on the "exterior senses,"[26] Aquinas makes a tripartite distinction between sight as the most "spiritual" sense, hearing and smelling as involving greater involvement with material objects, and taste and touch as the most material, since they are actually altered in contact with their proper objects. Hegel, similarly, makes a tripartite distinction between sight and hearing as the senses of physical "ideality," smell and taste as the senses of real corporeal decomposition, and touch as the sense of solid corporeal reality.

Both Aquinas and Hegel seem to be following a strategy used by Aristotle (in A-DeA II, 10)—differentiating the exterior senses according to their objects and the degree of materiality involved. But they depart from the Aristotelian categorization, especially with regard to the spirituality or ideality (or both) of the sense of sight.

A similar parallelism is noteworthy in regard to the differentiation of feelings or emotions. Aquinas, loosely following Aristotle, distinguishes three kinds of "interior senses": the aggressive "irascible" appetite, which leads humans to overcome difficulties; the "concupiscible" appetite, or desire for various types of pleasure; and the "cogitative power" (*vis cogitativa*), which bundles up the emotions and helps lead them in the direction of rational choices (Aquinas I,q78,a4; I,q81,a3; I–II,q74,a3). Hegel concentrates on the various ways in which the intertwining of soul and body lead to various sympathies/antipathies. Paralleling Aquinas's "concupiscible, irascible, and cogitative" appetites are Hegel's "desire in the reproductive organs, anger and endurance in the breast as the center of irritability, and thoughtfulness, spiritual concern, in the head, the center of the system of sensibility" (H3, §318). In Hegel's final version of his Philosophical Anthropology, he takes a more nuanced approach and introduces a hierarchy of inner feelings. Desire for pleasure and avoidance of the unpleasant are demoted and subordinated to the feelings most connected with spiritual awareness—that is, the feelings concerned with one's immediate individuality (anger, revenge, etc.), and inner feelings directed toward universality (emotional orientations to human rights, morality and religion) (E3, §401, Zusatz).

All such feeling-states manifest an intimate coordination of the spiritual and the corporeal, as befits these initial stages of anthropological life. But the subsequent states of antithesis or dysfunction (discussed below) are "higher" in a dialectical sense, insofar as they result from the further complexification of the human spirit, which has not yet arrived at its most "concrete" forms.

Dreaming, ESP, Hypnotism: The investigation of arcane phenomena such as dreaming and extrasensory perception presumably could throw some light on the relationship of mind to body and the scope and limits of conceptualization. Treatises on such subjects were rather commonplace in ancient and medieval philosophy; but in most branches of modern philosophy there has been little or no interest in them. A major exception, ironically, has been "analytic" philosophy, which prides itself on avoiding all forms of frivolous metaphysical speculation. Other branches of philosophy and schools of metaphysics, possibly still intimidated by Kant's stipulations about what can and cannot be known, generally avoid in-depth discussion of dreaming, hypnotism, or the paranormal.

Hegel's treatment of dreaming comes at the outset of the "antithetical" stage of Subjective Spirit, where the soul, which implicitly embraces all of reality, is just beginning to emerge from its immediacy, realize its differentiation from the world, and establish itself as universality (E3, §405–406). In order to explain how this happens, Hegel resorts to the notion of the "genius," in the classical sense—the highly individualized guardian spirit or "genie" common in mythology (in the form of guardian divinities, demons, oracles, etc.)—to express an inner particularization of circumstances constituting an individual's destiny. Hegel hypothesizes that in the prenatal period, the fetus is immediately affected by the feeling of the mother, who becomes the personification of the self the fetus is reaching out for (the "genius"). After birth, dreaming becomes a means by which the soul attains and continually reestablishes an *immediate* unity with its own concrete individuality or "genius," projected in a variety of ways. The dreamer is immersed in the total sense of his or her individuality, past, present and future; thus it is to be expected that no predictable relationship to ordinary chronological time is to be found in dreams.

In a reflective individual who has transcended the immediate unity with his or her "genius" and is progressing to a more mediated stage, various forms of morbid psychic dualism may result, so that the rational part is alienated from the sensitive part (E3, §406, Zusatz). This may help explain phenomena such as divination (discovering sources of water or metal below the ground without the ordinary use of the senses); somnambulism (in which a dream expresses itself in external activities such as walking, sometimes with a remarkable awareness of actual objects); and "clairvoyance."

Hegel uses "clairvoyance" as an umbrella term to refer to what we would describe as a resurfacing of unconscious memories or as various forms of extrasensory perception (ESP). He subdivides "clairvoyance" as follows: (1) ability to recall things or languages one has forgotten from childhood; (2) inner perception of purely external, unseen spatial happenings (i.e., "clairvoyance" in our contemporary sense of the term); (3) a contingent and sometimes vague apprehension of future happenings ("precognition," in current usage); (4) perception of one's own physical, mental or spiritual states, or knowledge of one's spiritual potentialities in the form of a "guardian angel"; (5) a similar perception of the states of other people; and (6) ability to *enter into* the feelings or states of other people. (States 5 and 6 would be characterized as "telepathy" in current usage.)

There was much lively discussion in Hegel's time about hypnotism (also called "mesmerism" and "animal magnetism"). The intermittent successes of Anton Mesmer (1734–1815) and his followers were accomplishments waiting for satisfactory theoretical explanations. Hegel took up this challenge, and he goes into considerable detail (E3, §406, Zusatz) trying to interpret the many cases, or alleged cases, in which hypnotic procedures were used successfully. He was particularly interested in the possibility that hypnotism could be used to cure various illnesses.

Hegel maintains that hypnotism is similar to ESP ("clairvoyance") insofar as it involves a primal psychic dualism, but it differs insofar as it is artificially and deliberately provoked. The hypnotist must have a superior, authoritative personality and must be able, by stroking, touching, or glancing, to produce psychic effects in weaker, more dependent people, and also in certain animals. "Faith healing" by priests or ministers is generally a form of this phenomenon. In order to be hypnotized, a subject need not be literally asleep but must be psychically asleep. The hypnotic trance itself seems to involve the withdrawal of the externally directed faculties of the mind into the "mind" of the vegetative system (autonomic nervous system); one could say that the subject's *being* withdraws into his or her innermost recesses. This gives subjects an ability to know their own hidden sicknesses, or sometimes to know about future world events, or things that they perceive in the mind of the hypnotist. But for some unknown reason, if paranormal powers are conferred through hypnotism, they cannot be used for personal gain—e.g., they could not be used to win a lottery.

Insanity: Hegel observes (E3, §408 and Zusatz) that in order to understand insanity, we first have to take into account the fact that the soul moving out of its state of corporeal immediacy is progressing toward *consciousness,* i.e., the state in which a dynamic, mediated relationship between subjectivity and objectivity will be attained. In approximating this goal, however, it is to be expected *dialectically* that an extreme separation of subjective from objective should take place at some point, before the final coordination of the extremes. The fact that this is a *dialectically* necessary development does not, however, imply that all individuals have to pass explicitly through this state. In fact, those who actually do arrive at this extreme are said to be "insane."

Insanity as a psychic disruption is quite analogous to physical disease. In a physical disease, such as cancer or hypertension, one part or element of the organism acts in disharmony with the whole; and if there is to be a cure, it consists in reestablishing harmony, reintegrating with the body as a whole the part that was acting in isolation. In mental disease, there is a semiconscious identification with some negative aspect of the self, a negative "genius," so to speak; this is "negative communion," something like a masochistic satisfaction in pain and suffering. The insane person fixes on some isolated feeling—e.g., that he or she is a king or queen, or a dog, or an object of persecution—in such a way that this idea is not coordinated with either objective reality or the complexus of the person's other ideas. Thus an insane person is like a sleepwalker who is trying to act out dreams; but the insane person, being driven by a dream while still awake, is in a higher and more complex state than the sleepwalker.

One of the most important things to understand about insanity is that it is not an "irrational" state; rather, it is an approximation to rationality in which the unfortunate patient has been arrested in a dual-personality syndrome, on the way to fully mediated consciousness. Thus, any possibility of successful treatment of insanity requires recognizing the patient's implicit rationality; and since the phenomenon of insanity takes place in a state where the psyche is extremely influenced by physical sensations and feelings, the approach to healing must be psychosomatic.

Hegel classifies the various mental diseases in terms of three possible discrepancies in the relationship between the patient's subjectivity and objective reality. (1) *Indeterminate self-engulfment.* In the first class of cases, an individual is locked into abstract subjectivity and is unable to interact with external reality or with other persons. Sometimes this is a result of congenital abnormalities (e.g, what used to be called "mongolism"); sometimes it is a temporary or permanent state triggered by unanticipated or traumatic experiences (e.g., depression or catatonia brought on by sudden loss of a loved one). Other examples of extreme self-absorption would include the "absentminded professor," the rambling minds of persons constantly muttering to themselves, and narcissism. (2) *Insanity in the strict sense—unreflective mode.* In the second type of case, a person not only is captivated by a subjective idea taken out of context but applies or projects that idea in objective reality, without being aware of any discordance. Examples would include a vague idea of the meaninglessness of life, leading to acute depression and disgust with everything in the objective world; or a definite idea that one is Christ or a king or queen, leading to delusions of grandeur. (3) *Insanity in the strict sense— reflective mode:* In a case of the third type, the insane person is not only possessed by a single idea which is at odds with reality but is aware of the contradiction involved and is driven to mania or frenzy by this awareness. Examples include schizophrenic alienation from reality, stubborn regression to one's past life because of unwillingness to accept the present, paranoiac behavior, and misanthropic aggressiveness toward others.

Again, it should be kept in mind that insanity is not a necessary stage that anyone has to transverse, but it does illustrate the necessary extremes that occur as the feeling soul makes the transition to conscious mediation with objectivity and to rationality.

Psychic integration: In the two opening sections of Hegel's discussion of anthropology, he takes up oppositions emerging in the embodied soul— either moderate forms of oppositions such as sleep-wakefulness and dream-reality, or the extreme oppositions of insanity. The necessary catalyst for overcoming these oppositions is *habit,* which he takes up in the third section. By means of habit, the soul begins to seize on the primary externality which confronts it (i.e., its body) and reduce that externality to unity and universality (E3, §410). The formation of habits is also a movement toward freedom, insofar as bodily impulses—e.g., standing, seeing, thinking, writing—become mechanical and of no immediate concern—but also, paradoxically, a matter of necessity, insofar as habit is "second nature."

Habit supplies the transition to the full *actuality* of soul, in which the soul raises corporeity to "ideality," i.e., a *mediated* unity-in-opposition (E3, §411–12, Remark). This actuality is expressed in various ways. To a lesser degree, it is expressed in human pathognomy (comparable to what is now called "body language"), and in physiognomy, which gives a more permanent expression to character or to a person's habitual passions or moods. Other human qualities, such as the ability to walk upright, the use of the hand as an "instrument of instruments," and the ability to laugh and cry—offer the soul additional avenues of expression and further accentuate the differentiation of the human soul from the soul of other animals. *Language and deeds,* however, give the most perfect and unambiguous portrayal of the ideality of soul. The soul, having attained these levels, is capable of becoming *Consciousness,* that is, a mediated opposition. As Consciousness, the soul will no longer be faced with inassimilable types of otherness but will find its "natural" expression (in the sense of "second nature") and its reflection in the objective world.

IV. Politics and the "Kingdom of God"

Plato, in common with all of his thinking contemporaries, recognizing the corruption of democracy and the deficiency of the very principle of democracy, brought into relief the substantial principle of the state; but he was not able to incorporate the infinite form of subjectivity in his idea of the state. This was still concealed from his spirit. Hence Plato's state is intrinsically *lacking any subjective freedom.* . . . It was not granted to Plato to be able to progress further and say that, as long as the true religion had not entered into the world and reigned in the states, the true principle of the state has not come into reality. . . . The principles of religious and ethical conscience coincide in the Protestant conscience—the free spirit knowing itself in its rationality and truth. The constitution and legislation, as well as their applications, have for their content the ethical principle and its unfolding; this ethicality proceeds, and can only proceed, from the truth of [the Protestant] religion, reestablished in its original principle, and thus for the first time real (E3, §552).

Theologians, like philosophers, are not noted for in-house agreement. But one area of considerable and long-standing consensus among both Catholic and Protestant theologians is the pivotal importance in Christianity of the concept of a "kingdom of God." There are over a hundred references to the "kingdom of God" or the "kingdom of heaven" in the gospels; and it seems clear that the historical Jesus understood his mission primarily in terms of announcing—or possibly bringing about—this "kingdom."

At this point, I have to hedge and use disjunctions like "or" and qualifiers like "possibly," because concerning the precise nature of the "kingdom of God" there is now and always has been considerable and heated controversy among Christian interpreters. Was the kingdom meant to come during the generation in which Jesus lived? The early Christians began to abandon that interpretation a few centuries after he died. Was the kingdom purely spiritual, or was it meant to free human beings from social and political oppression and establish justice on earth? Was the kingdom to be identified with the Church or with some community of believers transcending all established churches? Is the inauguration of the kingdom something that depends on human initiative and control, or is it completely dependent on the intervention of God in human history?

These are not theoretical questions of interest only to academicians. The meaning of the "kingdom of God" in western Christian (or "post-Christian") civilization is of the utmost importance for politics. It makes a great deal of difference, after all, whether we interpret the kingdom as a world empire, as a worldwide Christian republic, as a purified Christian community separate from the world, or as an apocalyptic event which will finally rescue the faithful from the ineluctable injustice of secular governments. Constantine's court theologian, Eusebius, interpreted it as a world empire; and so did Adolf Hitler, who in effect continued the Germanic "Holy Roman Empire" as the Third Reich—although Hitler, of course, eschewed the theological connotations. Dante interpreted it as a worldwide Christian republic; various monastic orders, and the Mennonites and Amish in our day, have thought of it as a separated, purified community; Jehovah's Witnesses and Seventh-Day Adventists think of it as an apocalypse.

In the post–World War II era, there have been new political-theological interpretations of the kingdom of God. These include the "moral majority" movement (now disbanded) in the United States, and the commitment (still continuing) to a social kingdom of God encapsulated in the periodical *Sojourner*. They also include the concept, held by many contemporary Zionists—including not only Jews but also some conservative Christian theologians—of finally acquiring the promised land.

Another interpretation is seen in the passionate revolutionary struggle to establish the ultimate reign of justice, advocated by Latin American liberation theologians and implemented in an inchoate way in "base communities" in many Latin American countries. A secularized but still recognizable form can be seen in Marxist movements, now in disarray and trying to regroup after having striven against considerable odds to establish—not in some future world but on this earth—a reign of peace and justice beyond capitalism, made possible by the emergence of a new, socialized species of humanity.

If one's theological interpretation of the kingdom of God has any political ramifications, they will of course be of the utmost importance for democracy. Someone who is committed to a particular idea of the kingdom may want to know whether his theological ideal is consistent with, and possibly even conducive to, democracy. Someone who is committed to democracy, on the other hand, should be interested in determining whether his political ideal is compatible with a long-standing and deep-rooted theological tradition, or must in some way distance itself from that tradition.

One initial obstacle in addressing such problems is the current, growing ambiguity of the term "democracy" itself. In recent times, almost every kind of government—with the exception of some out-and-out dictatorships—has called itself a "democracy." Karl Marx in 1843 hailed communism as the harbinger of true democracy; and in recent decades there have been various "people's democracies," "democratic republics," and the like, which are or were a long way from what the "western world" considers the essential criteria of democracy. The fact that many of these systems have now implemented "democratization" processes to counteract the Marxist version of "democracy" also sends us back to the drawing board. What does "democratization" mean? Does it require a free market? Are free elections a necessary and sufficient condition for "democracy"? Are constitutional checks and balances prerequisites of a stable democracy? And so forth. Jacques Barzun observes that the common-denominator meaning of "democracy" seems to be that "the people should be sovereign, and [that] this popular sovereignty implies political and social equality."[27] But this is perhaps too general. For in actual practice there is of course perpetual conflict, even in "democratic" systems, between equality and freedom; and "the people" does not have the same meaning now—in the aftermath of the nineteenth-century industrial revolutions and twentieth-century social revolutions, that it had in former eras.

In the eighteenth century, there was considerable diffidence among political theorists concerning the value of democracy. Rousseau came to the conclusion that full democratic participation after the model of the ancient Athenian polity was simply impossible in a large nation; and the authors of the American Constitution were so ambivalent about the term "democracy" that they insisted on characterizing the government they were founding more precisely, not as a "democracy" but as a "democratic republic." In our own world of nation-states, what is left over from the classical democracy of the Greek *polis* is that minimal residue of meaning which Jacques Barzun adumbrates: a very general, overly vague notion of the sovereignty of the people.

Hegel agreed substantially with Madison and Jefferson, as well as with Rousseau, Kant, and others: "democracy" *was* an unwieldy and impractical notion in the modern world. But instead of leaning, like the others, toward sublimating democracy and replacing it with the traditional ideal of a "republic," Hegel advocated a more radical restructuring of the political ideal in terms of the essential notion of a free modern society, based on the reconciliation of opposites in the Idea, and receiving fuller elaboration in his political philosophy.

Ancient Greek democracy, according to Hegel, was the political zenith of an era of *objective* spirit in which it so happened that the wills of individual citizens were intrinsically intertwined with the objective will manifested in the polity (PH, 306–07). The citizens had no conscience or "morality" in our modern sense; but they had virtue and *Sittlichkeit,* domestic and civic ethicality, and this prevented disharmony. The injection of subjectivity—as exemplified by the antiestablishment comedies of Aristophanes and the iconoclastic philosophizing of Socrates— destroyed the Greek spirit. Thus their kind of democracy is impossible in our own time, which is strongly characterized by subjectivity.

According to Hegel, Christianity, with its emphasis on the worth of the individual and on the right of subjectivity to be satisfied and fulfilled, renewed and intensified the question of subjectivity (PR, §124). But Christianity also pointed the way to a solution, through its doctrine of the Incarnation. The Incarnation—beyond its literal meaning, the advent of a man-God—was a symbol of the union of divine and human, subjective will and objective reality, freedom and nature, individual and community (HP2, 509–10.) The reconciliation of these opposites, and ultimately the reconciliation of God with himself, became, in Hegel's estimation, the leading idea of the Christian community, which perpetuated and perpetuates a communal reenactment of the death and resurrection of the man-god throughout history. Although the Christian church was not always or even generally a worthy instrument for the accomplishment of this ideal, it did serve as a prephilosophical custodian of the synthesizing Absolute Idea, down through the centuries.

It is true, says Hegel, that the Roman Catholic Church quickly began to appropriate for itself political power, as soon as it rose from the second-class status it had under the Roman empire. Then it began to build up a quasi-empire of its own, an "ecclesiastical kingdom of God" which lorded it over secular authorities and secular existence, intermittently attempting to control the state either by force or by creating a division between church-related political parties and parties that were not church-related (HP, 402).[28] Nevertheless, he points out, such political excesses were simply a manifestation of the imperfect development within Catholicism of the Christian idea, which instead of achieving freedom kept humanity in a kind of spiritual slavery, oriented toward the mere externals of spirituality under a pseudospiritual leadership imbued more with the secular spirit than with the spirit of God (E3, §356–57).[29]

But finally, Hegel tells us, with the advent of Protestantism, the church awoke to its truly spiritual but essentially private calling. The vocation of the church is, after all, something quite private. This does not mean "private" in a pejorative sense—that is, in the sense that Catholicism had been able to stand aloof from and indifferent to countless abuses in the secular sphere (PRe1, 241–44). Rather, it means private in the sense that in the world the church is a hidden source, a divine springboard for all authentic moral activity in the public sphere (E3, 365). The inner kingdom of God, as conceived by Hegel, is a direct "vertical" relationship to the divine, and its "horizontal" correlate is the state—that ultimate community, the ethical and juridical arena where alone divine freedom and truth can be fully realized and guaranteed (PH, 502; HP2, 509).[30] It has to be kept in mind that the state, as Hegel construes it, is not an organization but a massive organism, in almost a literal sense (E3, §§542, 544); and religion is the inner life, the soul, of that organism, more fundamental even than morality.

It would be a serious mistake to ignore or underestimate the important function of religion in Hegel's concept of the state. Hegel, like Kant, viewed politics as a derivation from, and an extension of, the moral order; but Hegel went beyond Kant in basing the moral order itself in religion, and specifically, in the modern world, in Protestant Christianity.

Protestantism is not only the foundation for moral and just interpersonal relations, but the indispensable means for building up the entire edifice of secular relations within the state (PH, 502). In the last analysis, it is religion that supplies the grounding for the organization of modern free states and their laws (PH, 494; Pre2, 332; EIII, §552). Under Protestantism, according to Hegel, there was no longer any need for the cyclical but incessant conflict between "church and state" or their alienation from each other; for Protestantism itself was the realization—albeit an abstract realization—of the final reconciliation of the political and the religious (E3, 365; see also PH, 502, PRe1, 241–44).

One might reasonably suppose that a *democracy* rooted in Protestant Christianity would best meet Hegel's criteria. Does not democracy, even in Jacques Barzun's common-denominator meaning, incorporate subjectivity to a high degree, and take steps to ensure the fair representation of personhood at the highest levels of government? Yes, of course. But in Hegel's mind democracy is only an imperfect step in the right direction. Hegel, no doubt thinking of Rousseau's political philosophy, castigates democracy for offering just one more *quantitative* solution to the problem of the representation of subjectivity; in other words, a democracy, instead of representing only one or a few subjectivities, represents a majority of personhood-units. He disapproves of democracy also for inculcating a simplistic, mathematical, idea of human equality—in contemporary terms, "one man, one vote" (PR, §§49, 200, 273). Such a "solution," in Hegel's view, is incapable of dealing with the truly qualitative problems presented by subjectivity in the modern world. Democratic constitutions are in the final analysis overly cerebral constructions of spirit, depending on artificial devices like "separation of powers" and "checks and balances" to stave off the self-destructiveness of what is essentially an unhealthy adversary relationship. And they aim at a utopian equality, which can be reached only in the spiritual realm, in the kingdom of God:

> The soul, the individual subjectivity, has an infinite, *eternal vocation:* to be a citizen in the kingdom of God. . . . The subjectivity that has comprehended its infinite value has therewith given up all distinctions of mastery, of power, of class, even of sex: before God all persons are equal. In the negativity of the infinite pain of love there lies also the initial potentiality and root of genuine universal rights, the *realization of freedom* (PRe2, 303).

An inception of this ideal equality on earth is to be found, it is true, in Protestant Christianity,[31] and democracy, at its best, is attempting to implement this equality in the political sphere. But democracy is simply incapable of dealing with the complexities of modern subjectivity, of guaranteeing the maximum qualitative representation of individuals who may be spiritually equal but manifest all manner of natural and material differences in any empirical society. In fact, the subjective valuation of liberty which is characteristic of modern consciousness is bound to cause progressive increases in *in*equalities which are beyond the leveling influences of democracy (E3, §539, Remark).

The solution in Hegel's philosophy is not to ignore differences, but to focus on the essential categorial differences; that is, to develop political relations in conformity with the speculative-dialectical "Idea" of the unity of opposites, which in politics translates into an intrinsic reconciliation of objective order and subjective aspiration, necessity and freedom, nature and spirit. In conformity to this Idea, the state should correspondingly be based and built up on the various "natural" divisions of the subjectivities which compose it—classes, "estates," unions, and associations, as well as majorities[32]—so that freedom can be strengthened and perpetuated by being rooted in what is natural and inevitable. In accord with the same principles, Hegel, as is well-known, opted for a constitutional monarchy, in which the monarch's natural individuality and familial succession to the throne would be coordinated with the spiritual excogitations of parliamentary government, as the final unifying device in a free society. An additional "natural" support would be a bicameral legislature: one house consisting of landed gentry, who would presumably be a stabilizing influence, while the "deputies" in the other house would represent the various divisions created in civil society by the more mobile progressions of Spirit.

We should not be too hasty in dismissing Hegel's royalist critique of democracy as reactionary and outdated. Although we may view "coordination of nature and spirit" as a problem that only an adamant German idealist could think up and try to solve, situations frequently do arise in the world's democracies in which we might wish for something very much like the bolstering of nature itself to prop up the institutions and policies devised by the rational spirits of incumbent governments. A Hegelian might want to compare the astounding stability and security through thick and thin of a constitutional monarchy like that in England with the instability and chaotic successions of the parliamentary democracy in Italy; or point with disdain at the frequent prolonged neglect of business by governments like the United States' during elections in which the incumbent president is a candidate; and, finally, top off this critique with a smug comment about the quality of the president (no names, please) who emerges from the interminable electoral processes. But one does not have to be a hypercritical monarchist to ask: if it would not be a boon to any free, democratic society to bring in nature as an ever-present support of spirit through natural groupings and what Hegel called "corporations"—municipalities, economic associations, professional groups, labor organizations, religious congregations, and the like. And might not Hegel be right at least in his general observation that the Protestant church (and perhaps even a suitably protestantized Catholicism!) can and perhaps must be a spiritual ally of the state in fostering the concepts of individual freedom, personal morality and responsibility, and freedom of thought (PR, §270), which are important for creating a government that would be activated more by initiative from below than coercion from above?

On the other hand, Hegel's position has important structural defects which even a critic of democracy should be aware of. For one thing, monarchy is a rather arbitrary way of uniting nature with freedom in political administration. The odds are astronomical against a royal family's producing talented and concerned scions generation after generation; and, as Theunissen points out, a monarch whose mission is to unite nature and spirit is a Christ-figure in Hegel's schema—a role which most monarchs, even in Hegel's time, would presumably not consciously aspire to, let alone be capable of (Theunissen 447). It is also quite conceivable that other, more satisfactory ways of "uniting nature and spirit" than monarchy could be devised with some minimal effort and ingenuity. For example, would not a meritocracy, requiring tests for aptitude, intelligence, and experience as a prerequisite for being elected to the highest government offices, be a logical, albeit complicated, way of coordinating natural ability with the determinations of "spirit"? Or one could reasonably maintain, along with Alexis de Tocqueville, that the perennial division in politics into conservative and liberal camps is not just an accident of history, but something intrinsic to political systems—a "natural" division whose recognition and institutionalization is a prerequisite for modern enlightened politics.

But in a more fundamental sense, can we not argue forcibly that democracy itself is precisely the sort of union of nature and spirit that someone like Hegel might be looking for? Democracy joins the organizational forces of government with the sine qua non of voluntary initiative and participation by the governed—the sort of thing that erstwhile communist governments have belatedly been trying to inculcate through "democratization." In a somewhat similar vein, Hartmann thinks that Hegel could have elaborated a sound idealistic political theory based on a republican rather than a monarchical constitution (Hartmann 62, 101, 575ff.). The real philosophical problem for Hegel and Hegelians, Hartmann observes, is to bring about a synthesis of the rational-speculative "Category" in Hegel's system with anthropology. Such a synthesis would be necessary in order to demonstrate just *how* an existential "communion" of citizens can be conjoined with the reason and organicity emphasized in Hegel's system (Hartmann 577–78). Hösle suggests that if the discrete atomization of a self-interested citizenry is the major obstacle to political synthesis, political parties themselves may function as organic structures mediating between particular individuals and the "universals" of government (Hösle 579).

But let us put aside for the moment questions about whether or not a democratic or republican government might be a better way, *pace* Hegel, to bring about the ideal of a free society. Granted that a free society and a free state are ideals that we share with Hegel, what is to be said about Hegel's proposal for overcoming the counterproductive adversary relationship between religion and government (which had characterized Catholic eras) by creating a new cooperative and complementary relationship? In the aftermath of the undoubted benefits that have been derived by separating various denominations from *each other* (PR, §270), should the relation of church and state be an "inseparable union" (E3, §552) in the context of the Absolute Idea? We of course have the considerable advantage of hindsight in answering that question. We know, for example, that the Protestantism whose spirit of freedom Hegel prized was no bulwark of individual freedom in Germany during the era of National Socialism. And Catholics can scarcely feel superior in this respect, since they by and large also kept silence—a German bishop achieved a last-minute "success" by preventing Pope Pius XI from issuing a public warning against Hitler's anti-Semitism. And Nazi Germany, of course, is just one example. At the end of the twentieth century, we have a sufficiently broad outlook on the history of close unions between politics and religion (whether Protestant, Catholic or non-Christian) to know that too close a relationship can be at least as deleterious as its opposite. In any case, it is obviously in the area of church-state relations that Hegel's interpretation of the "kingdom of God" becomes most crucial and fundamental. And this is the subject on which our final attention should be focused.

Protestants, for rather obvious reasons, have been reluctant to accept Augustine's assertion that the visible church is the "present kingdom of

God" preparing the way for the "end times." To the Augustinian monk
Martin Luther, as well as to his religious successors, it was obvious that
to associate the "kingdom of God" with the visible church would be to
forfeit the possibility of reform and to compromise with the then-pre-
vailing virulent abuses of religion and religious authority. Hegel, as a
convinced Lutheran, was likewise unwilling to locate the source of spiritual freedom in the Catholic Church—which, he observed, although
experiencing a thrust toward democracy in the traditional processes of
electing the pope, had become by and large a bastion of aristocratic
conservatism through the power of priestly consecration. A church
with a spiritual elite standing far above the secular world could never
be an appropriate vehicle for, or a perpetuator of, "infinite" freedom:
concrete rather than abstract self-determination in the world and in
secular society.

Catholicism aside, Hegel did, however, share with Augustine the
opinion (now extremely controversial among theologians) that the
church is the present kingdom of God (PH, 401; HP2, 409–10).[33] But
for Hegel this presence is manifested not in an ecclesiastical organization, but by its spiritual influence on social and public life:

> The church is the kingdom of God, the *achieved* presence, *life and mainte-*
> *nance* and enjoyment of the Spirit. . . . Family, property, temporal con-
> cerns arise on their own—and laws and governance; the essential thing
> here is that out of the womb of the church A FREE civil and political life
> is cultivated on the basis of ETERNAL PRINCIPLES, a *rational* secular
> realm, consonant with *the Idea of freedom,* and the absoluteness of rights.
> Insofar as the law, the rational, the universal belongs to the secular in
> this way, what remains for the church is the salvation of the individual
> soul, the particular subjectivity; the secular universality takes care of
> itself.[34]

Hegel's position has elicited considerable criticism for its facile identification of present with eschaton and secular with sacred (see, e.g., Theunissen 441). Hegel also poses a problem for theologians and practitioners of political theology. Let us suppose that the kingdom of God is
present but *not* to be identified with any visible church: in what sense,
then—and where—is it present? Hegel possibly gives the most plausi-
ble answer to this question quite straightforwardly in the passage just
cited: it is located in the inner sanctum of subjectivity, a reservoir of spiritual resources springing up from private depths and quietly transforming public life and political relationships. How does it do this? Not by

church activity or liturgy, not by lobbying for religious causes, and not by seeking converts, but simply by producing an everyday reconciliation of the spiritual and the secular in ordinary life by means of individuals who have already brought about a foundational reconciliation of the spiritual and the secular within their own personalities. All in all, we find in Hegel a decisive and concerted effort to counterbalance what he considered the alienation found in the history of the relationship of the Christian religion to the world. But does he not go too far in the other direction?

It should be remembered that not only was Hegel a product of his time; he also thought a philosopher had no choice *but* to be a product of his time (PR, 26)—and presumably he was quite satisfied with this limitation on philosophizing. But if philosophers are indeed products of their own time, we in our time at least have the benefit of an extra 150 years history—a history which includes the phenomena of compliant Christians under Nazism, a largely cooperative Orthodox Church under Bolshevism, nationalistic Protestantism and Catholicism in Ireland, militant politicized Islam in Iran, etc. To repeat a point made above, the unavoidable conclusion for someone objectively surveying the empirical past since Hegel's era would simply have to be that too close a unity (even noninstitutional) between church and state is as great a mistake as institutionalized conflict or jockeying for power between the two.

European theologians, perhaps influenced by the flawed history of attempts to erect the kingdom of God, and its corresponding "Reichs," on earth, have by and large adopted an eschatological interpretation of the Kingdom. European commentators, following the lead of Albert Schweitzer and others, tend toward "consistent eschatology"—the idea that all gospel references to the Kingdom have to be understood as references to a future coming. The Kingdom is something to be attained at the "end time," through the intervention of God, certainly not something to be produced in neo-Pelagian fashion by initiatives and organization on the part of the church. American theologians, in contrast, have until recently tended toward "realized eschatology"—the notion that the kingdom of God came with the coming of Christ, with the spiritual power that Christ in his life manifested over the forces of evil. Some theologians have tried to combine both positions—future and present eschatology—without contradiction. But the general picture we are presented with is one of continuing theological controversy.

The problem of defining the appropriate relationship between church and state may be most formidable for Protestant theologians, for whom the choice between a visible and an invisible church is a dilemma. On the one hand, scandals in the visible church were the impetus for the emergence of Protestantism in the first place. On the other hand, a strictly invisible, strictly private church, if it has anything to do with the inauguration of a kingdom of God on earth, must, it would seem, have to do so by default, in and through the most formidable earthly power, the state. But if the church is construed as in some sense a visible organization—not just a multiplicity of sects and denominations, any of which may be propagating true or false Christianity—then there still is, of course, the problem of distancing and clearly differentiating it (the "one true reformed church") from that ancient and clearly visible organization whose perceived abuses gave rise to Protestantism.

V. History and Providence

Karl Löwith, in his discussion of the emergence of the philosophy of history as a distinct discipline, argues that the Christian idea of divine providence gradually gave way, around the time of the Enlightenment in France and elsewhere, to the secularized notion that there is a kind of inevitable progress in history toward what is better and better.[35] He includes Hegel among the "secularizers" along with Voltaire, Condorcet, Turgot and other philosophers. Löwith casts their accomplishments in a negative light. What is this belief in endless progress but an inauthentic transference of the Christian belief in the coming of God's kingdom to the purely secular sphere? Intellectuals who found it difficult to believe in a final spiritual kingdom have, in Löwith's estimation, settled on a new, worldly belief that humanity is progressing in every way—scientifically, technologically, culturally, even morally.

Immanuel Kant would not have shared Löwith's misgivings. Living in the midst of the changes which Löwith castigates from a twentieth-century vantage point, Kant was much more sanguine about the value of the Enlightenment concept of progress. In his *Philosophy of History,* Kant presents progress as a viable and compatible rational counterpart of the religious idea of divine providence, and as concerned specifically with the inevitable evolution of the nations of the world toward peace:

> Here . . . is a proposition valid for the most rigorous theory, in spite of all skeptics, and not just a well-meaning and practically commendable proposition: The human race has always been in progress toward the better and will continue to be so henceforth. To him who does not consider what happens in just some one nation but also has regard to the whole

scope of all the peoples on earth who will gradually come to participate in progress, this reveals the prospect of an immeasurable time. . . . The hope for [the human race's] progress is to be expected only on the condition of a wisdom from above (which bears the name of Providence if it is invisible to us); but for that which can be expected and exacted from *men* in this area toward the advancement of this aim, we can anticipate only a negative wisdom, namely, that they will see themselves compelled to render [war] firstly by degrees more humane and then rarer, and finally to renounce offensive war altogether, in order to enter upon a constitution which . . . can persistently progress toward the better.[36]

Löwith, in sharp contrast, finds this conceptual conjunction of "progress" (even construed as "negative wisdom") with "providence" regrettable—a watering-down of the religious experience of transcendence inculcated by Christianity, a dismaying orientation of human life to purely secular aspirations and expectations—overoptimistic expectations doomed to generate disappointment when they inevitably fall short of fulfillment.

During the last century, the idea of constant progress has often been coupled with evolution, even though Darwin's theory of "natural selection" eschews any teleological interpretations, including expectations of progress. Nevertheless, some proponents of social evolution, branching off sharply from Darwin, have explicitly extrapolated the idea of the upward biological progress in the tree of evolution into overarching concepts of social or moral progress, or both. A recent example is the French Jesuit paleontologist and philosopher, Teilhard de Chardin, who observes:

We are sometimes inclined to think that the same things are monotonously repeated over and over again in the history of creation. That is because the season is too long by comparison with the brevity of our individual lives, and the transformation too vast and too inward by comparison with our superficial and restricted outlook, for us to see the progress of what is tirelessly taking place in and through all matter and all spirit.[37]

A similar theory of ethical and spiritual evolution is propounded by M. Scott Peck in his best-selling book, *The Road Less Travelled:*

The notion that the plane of mankind's spiritual development is in a process of ascension may hardly seem realistic to a generation disillusioned with the dream of progress. Everywhere is war, corruption and pollution. How could one reasonably suggest that the human race is spiritually progressing? Yet that is exactly what I suggest. Our very sense of disillusionment arises from the fact that we expect more of ourselves than our forebears did of themselves. Human behavior that we find repugnant and outrageous today was accepted as a matter of course yesteryear.[38]

Hegel, if he were living today, would probably agree with such progressive views—to Löwith's dismay. But Hegel's reasoning would be based on different premises from Teilhard's or Peck's; and Hegel would proffer a different interpretation of the final goal toward which humanity is progressing. Hegel would also characterize Löwith's "secularization hypothesis" as an unsubtle oversimplification of his approach, and resolutely deny that he had any intention to do away with Christian transcendence. To understand why this is so, we have first to take into account Hegel's unique general optimism about the interrelationship of Christianity and modern philosophy, and more specifically the power of philosophical conceptualization to bring out the true meaning of Christian dogmas.

> The authority of the canonical faith of the church has been partly submerged, partly eliminated. Even the Creed, the rule of faith, is no longer accounted as strictly binding, but as something that is interpreted and explained from the Bible. But interpretation is dependent on the spirit that is explaining; the absolute footing [for interpretation] is only the Concept[39] In contrast to this footing, by means of exegesis such basic doctrines of Christendom are partly set aside, partly subjected to lukewarm explanations. Such dogmas as that of the Trinity and miracles are placed in the shadows by theology itself. The justification of these dogmas, their authentic formulation, can only take place through the cognizing Spirit. Thus there is much more dogmatics contained in philosophy than in Dogmatics proper, in theology itself *qua* theology.[40]

Here, Hegel is echoing St. Anselm's *credo ut intelligam* ("I believe in order to understand")—faith as the foundation for speculative philosophizing. The highest speculative truths are contained implicitly in Christian dogmas such as the Trinity; and philosophy, or "Absolute Knowledge," as Hegel observes in his *Phenomenology of Spirit* (PSK, §802), begins with the imaginative, figurative truths of religion as its indispensable content; these truths are imperfect only insofar as they still need to be elaborated into suitable rational-conceptual formulations. A major part of Hegel's system of philosophy is concerned precisely with such speculative elaboration of religious ideas. Thus Hegel describes his *Phenomenology of Spirit* as the "Golgotha of Absolute Spirit" (PS, 531), his *Science of Logic* as the conceptualization of the "life of God before the creation of the world" (SL1 44), and the political sections of his *Philosophy of Right* as "the march of God through the world" (PR, §258, Zusatz). Thus also Hegel's Philosophy of History is a rational-conceptual elaboration of the Christian concept of divine providence. Hegel states this in the initial sections of *Lectures on the Philosophy of History,* where he begins with a criticism of theologians. He cites the scriptural injunction that we should "*know,* love and serve God," and then goes on to observe that

> In our day things have gotten so bad in theology that philosophy has had to espouse the cause of the content of religion against various brands of theology. In the Christian religion, God has revealed himself; this means that He has entrusted to humans the power of knowing what He is, so that He is no longer something hidden and secret. Along with this possibility of knowing God, the duty of doing so is also imposed on us. God does not want any faint-spirited souls and empty heads among his children; he wants those who, albeit poor in spirit, are nevertheless rich in knowledge of Him and place all their emphasis on this knowledge alone. The development of the thinking spirit that proceeds on this foundation of the revelation of the divine Being must ultimately expand to comprehend in thought what initially is presented to its feeling and imagination (PH, 29).

Hegel then proceeds to apply this general optimism about the powers of human knowledge to the Christian doctrine of divine providence:

> The moment must eventually come for comprehending even that rich production of creative Reason which is world-history. It was the vogue for a while to admire God's wisdom as displayed in animals, plants, and individual destinies. If it is conceded that Providence is revealed in such objects and subject-matters, why not also in world-history? . . . [In response to this challenge,] our treatment of world-history is a theodicy, a justification of the ways of God (the sort of thing that Leibniz in his fashion attempted metaphysically, but with indeterminate, abstract categories), in order that the evil in the world might be understood, and the thinking Spirit reconciled with it. In reality nowhere is the need for such reconciling knowledge greater than in world-history. (PH, 28; see also E3, §564)

Hegel thus considers it an appropriate contribution of a philosopher in western Christian civilization, such as himself, to *demonstrate* the rationality of history—a rationality that is merely implicitly assumed by the theologians. And it will be noticed in the passage just cited that Hegel explicitly differentiates his approach from a natural-history approach. Unlike Marx, Huxley, Nietzsche, Spengler, and Spencer, who in very diverse ways tried to extrapolate the theory of organic evolutionary progress into the social and cultural realms, Hegel, who explicitly rejects the possibility of physical evolution (see above, page 88), concerns himself with the specifically spiritual evolution of mankind. His philosophy of history, looking for the "rose in the cross," for the essential rationality of historical reality, hypothesizes an ongoing evolution spearheaded by the development of the Concept of the state. The upward thrust of spiritual evolution, according to Hegel's theory, has to do with the gradual but inevitable emergence of human freedom in the modern state. He explains this in the Introduction to his Philosophy of History:

> The [ancient] Orientals still do not realize that Spirit, i.e. humanity as such, is free; and because they don't know this, they are not free; all they know is that *one person* is free, and thus their "freedom" is merely caprice, barbarity, aimless passion, or a tamed passion that is just an accident of nature, a matter of chance. Their "one free person" is thus himself a mere despot, not a free man. It is with the Greeks that the consciousness of freedom first emerged, and thus they were free; but they, and the Romans also, knew only that some people are free, not that human beings as such are free. Even Plato and Aristotle did not realize this. That is why the Greeks not only had slaves and had their life and the maintenance of their beautiful liberty tied up with slavery, but also this liberty itself was partly just a contingent, transitory and limited blossoming of freedom, partly at the same time a servitude of humanity and the human in general. It is the nations of the Western world that first arrived in Christendom at the consciousness that humans *qua* humans are free, and that freedom of Spirit constitutes their nature in the most proper sense. . . . The history of the world is the progress in the consciousness of freedom—a progress which we [in our philosophical study of history] have to understand in its necessity. (PH, 31–32)

"It is the nations of the Western world that first arrived in Christendom at the consciousness. . . ." Christendom? Establishing the spiritual environment for freedom? Hegel is operating, of course, at the antipode of Nietzsche's interpretation of Christianity as a "slave mentality." Christianity in Hegel's interpretation, far from inducing a slave mentality, is the fundamental source for the emergence in historical consciousness of the concept of freedom. How does Hegel come to this conclusion? The "middle term" for this connection of Christianity with free-dom is the unique emphasis in Christianity on *subjectivity*. The Christian idea of God as Absolute Being/Object, says Hegel, is expressly geared, in contrast to other religions, to accommodate the *subjective* element (E1, §194). The Christian God is an absolute, unique, free, personal subject. The notion of "liberty," in our modern sense of the word, did not even exist before Christianity came into the world (E3, §482). Although the practice of slavery ceased only gradually in Christianity (PH, 31), the idea that all human beings were equally free has been present in the world just since the beginning of the Christian era (E1, §163, Zusatz).

It is important to recall, however, as discussed in the previous section, that the ascent of the world toward a greater extensivity of freedom did not imply, in Hegel's mind, a trend toward *democracy*. The ideal of free-dom which supplies the motive force for all historical progress is "absolute freedom" (PR, §21ff.), a paradoxical concept of freedom which Hegel borrows in part from Fichte. Absolute freedom goes beyond abstract notions of freedom as "the ability to do as one wishes as long as one does not interfere with the freedom of others," or even as "the right to fulfil one's moral duties" or "autodetermination." In a state of absolute freedom, individuals are not just free; they *determine* themselves to be free—that is, they build up constitutional incentives and safe-guards so iron-tight that they almost, in Rousseau's words, *force* them-selves to be free.

The constitutional monarchy that Hegel defended was oriented, through instruments conducive to parliamentary consensus, and through various supports from "nature" such as the traditions of peer-age, toward predictable and stable communal progress in freedom. One might argue that the founders of the United States of America had the same objective in mind—"forcing" people to be free through objective institutions—but pursued this objective in a diametrically opposite way. The system of "checks and balances" emphasized in the American Con-stitution, establishing an adversarial relationship between the executive, legislative, and judicial branches of government, strives in a more nega-tive fashion to guarantee the freedom of all. What Hegel called the "judgement of history" will ultimately decide what political formation is most conducive to "absolute freedom"—possibly some variation beyond both constitutional monarchy and democracy. But the constant amid the variables, if Hegel's theory is correct, is that political experimenta-tion with objective guarantees of freedom will continue until all human beings are free, and that this state of affairs will ultimately come about.

As is well-known, Hegel compared philosophy to the owl of Minerva, which came out only at the end of day, looking back at the past, and having no privileged knowledge of the future. Hegel officially abjured prophecy, although he occasionally made some "off the record" guesses about what the future would hold—for example, his suggestion in his Philosophy of History that America would be the "land of the future." But what if Hegel could be present now, at the end of the twentieth century, and still have the benefit of the retrospective view which he thought so necessary to philosophy? Would he still adhere to his theory about the spiritual evolution toward freedom in history? How would he react to the almost universal demise of monarchies, even constitutional monarchies? In the wake of fascism and communism and the multiple genocides witnessed by our generation, would he be able to salvage his theory about the progression of freedom?

Hegel was not averse to revising his theories, when this was needed, as has been noted in an earlier chapter.[41] As we have seen in the previous section, it is conceivable that the Hegelian free state might be salvaged in nonmonarchical forms, as long as the union of nature and Spirit, essential to the idea of Absolute Freedom, could be maintained. The principal *realphilosophische* question Hegel would need to ask is this: are the natural divisions of society and the diverse gifts and callings of human subjectivity adequately represented at the level of the higher echelons of government? Possibly Hegel would find the contemporary Bundesrepublik Deutschland and other European social democracies—or even the United States of America—to be exemplars spearheading the historical progression of the concept of freedom.

It should be emphasized that when Hegel speaks about the "rationality" of history, he is not referring to some sort of logical consistency or predictability that could be distilled from an examination of historical events. Rather, here—as often—he is using "rationality" in the technical sense, referring to a unity-in-distinction of subjectivity and objectivity. The thrust of history, if Hegel is correct, is to bring about greater and greater coordination of subjectivities with the objective institutions and functions of the nation-state. This sort of "progress" can be compatible with dialectical oscillations and setbacks—in one place (PH, 35), Hegel refers to history as a "shambles")—as long as levels of rapprochement are progressively achieved. And if we want to gauge the progress that has been made in this rapprochement, our focus must be on the massive "organism" of the nation-state.

In the interest of the spiritual progress of mankind, would Hegel, even with the benefit of twentieth-century hindsight, ever be able to raise his sights *beyond* the parameters of the nation-state? Probably not. For Hegel, the free modern nation-state is where all of history has been heading. Hösle argues that Hegel distanced himself from nationalistic tendencies (Hösle 582n), but Hegel's trenchant critique of the famous proposal for a league of nations in Kant's treatise *Perpetual Peace* (PR, §333) smacks of nationalism, and indicates quite clearly that Hegel, unlike Kant, did not conceive of any final development of Absolute Freedom in the *international* sphere. In his rejection of Kant's vision, he no doubt anticipated the immense and possibly insuperable challenges facing the contemporary world, when it comes to implementing ideals of freedom beyond the parameters of the nation-state.

VI. Absolute Knowledge and Spirit

A. Absoluteness

References to the "absolute" in philosophy (or elsewhere) commonly conjure up in our minds concepts such as infinite series in mathematics, an infinite space containing the universe or multiple universes, a supreme being separate from and independent of the material universe, or possibly an ultimate peak of consciousness in which one experiences a gnostic penetration of all there is to know. Hegel's idea of the absolute has to be distinguished from such connotations. As indicated in earlier chapters (see pages 64 and 77), Hegel focuses on an absolute synthesis of subject and object, the "Idea"—corresponding to what Schelling called the "point of indifference," and effectively superseding all the Cartesian and Kantian dichotomies between ego and existence, consciousness and "thing in itself."

The "Absolute Knowledge" to which social and religious consciousness rises at the end of Hegel's *Phenomenology of Spirit* is by definition a type of knowledge in which there is no longer any split between knower and object. If we ask about Absolute Knowledge, "What is it knowledge *of?*" the only answer in Hegelian terms is that it is knowledge of Spirit. But Spirit itself is not an object but a fusion of subject and object; so, more precisely, Absolute Knowledge is not knowledge in the sense of a relation to some object, but a merger with Spirit, or Spirit's self-knowledge in and through human consciousness. Correspondingly, in the *Encyclopedia,* Absolute Spirit as the culmination of Hegel's system is not some ultimate universal object of knowledge; it is essentially knowledge cognizant of itself, or the knowledge of knowledge. Although Hegel in his later system takes up items that seem to fall into the category of subject or object—being, quality, space, time, color, sensation, feeling, thought—he always treats them in the context of the subjective-objective [S/O] Idea. Being is suffused with the abstract indeterminate thought that makes it equivalent to nothingness; space as an object gives rise to multiple paradoxes of sensation and perception; sensation as a subjective operation emerges from its organic roots in relation to a material environment; and so forth. Absolute Spirit in the *Encyclopedia* is simply the most explicit subjective-objective synthesis.

Some approximations to Absolute Spirit in the *Encyclopedia* have already been discussed. In Hegel's Philosophical Anthropology, his analysis of the experiences of the embodied soul in sensation, dreaming, emotional development, etc. remained on the interface between subjectivity and objectivity, proposing theories to explain the interrelationship between the two poles. In Hegel's political philosophy, we saw that his theory concerning constitutional monarchy was based on considerations about the necessity for uniting Nature and Spirit to produce a type of polity in which Nature itself would give constant support to the spiritual efforts of a nation to produce a free and stable society. But these were partial fusions. The complete fusion of subjectivity and objectivity is to be found only where Spirit in and through humankind rises to the highest level of self-consciousness. This takes place in art, religion and philosophy.

B. Art

In art, the S/O fusion is immediate. In any form or stage of art, there is no chance of isolating subjectivity or objectivity. The distinguishing characteristic of an "art object" is that it is not just an object; if we want to intuit the merger of subjectivity and objectivity, art gives us the best example of objects which are transformed by subjectivity. Both from a the passive viewpoint of the encounter with an aesthetic object and from the perspective of the creative artist forming an object and transplanting his visions into it, the fusion is complete.

Hegel distinguishes three forms of art—symbolic, classical and romantic—which correspond loosely (with numerous exceptions and qualifications) with the pre-Hellenic, Hellenic, and post-Hellenic periods, and with the concomitant evolution of forms of religion within these periods.

Symbolic art predominated in the oriental world, Egypt, and India. It was characterized by the use of materials and objects which were meant to give an immediate impression of striving after an indefinite Ideal,[42] an expansion of human horizons into the incommensurability of the divine (AES1, 108). For example, the pyramids and obelisks of ancient Egypt, and the massive figure of the Sphinx, by means of their size and configuration, symbolized nature's relationship to an inner life that was yet to be grasped (AES1, 459–60). Hindu depictions of the gods with multiple arms, legs, or heads were similar attempts to approximate an adequate expression of the Absolute with limited materials (AES1, 437). In all such cases, the immediate fusion of the objective with the subjective is apparent, but with an emphasis on the objective symbol.

In classical art, best exemplified in ancient Greek culture and religion, the Idea finally receives the shape proper to it and no longer outstrips its material embodiments (AES1, 108). What is signified, for instance, in Greek sculpture, is not something foreign to nature but a meshing of subjectivity and objectivity, nature and Spirit, especially in the human form (AES2, 13; E3, §558); Greek epics, lyric poems and dramas carry out the same anthropomorphic purposes in more spiritual media (AES3, 228). Classical art could be called the "absolute art" (although Hegel does not use that term) insofar as it portrays an S/O harmonization better than any other form of art. For us moderns, for whom these are just "works of art," it is difficult or impossible to understand the spiritual or religious experience of transcendence that the statue of a god in a temple or a dramatic performance would evoke in the ancient Greek consciousness. Thus in a sense there has been a "death" of art; art in the postmedieval "western," Christian world has lost its transcendent power, and in that sense has come to an end (PS, 490:24–491:26; AES1, 24).[43]

The kind of art that began to emerge in the Middle Ages and has come to full blossom in the modern world is romantic art, in which the immediate fusion of subjectivity and material media still prevails, but subjective factors stand out and overshadow objective factors. Romantic art emphasizes interiority, moods, feeling, love, and fidelity and the complications that result from these emotions (AES2, 169–94)—subjects that were peripheral to classical art. The spirit, personality, sufferings, and triumphs of religious and royal figures, saints, knights, lovers, and others, constitutes the common subject matter of romantic art, particularly in the specifically "romantic" arts—painting, music, and poetry (treated at length in AES3).

C. Religion

In classical art, the perfection in terms of an *immediate sensuous* S/O synthesis opens up the possibility of a *mediated* type of synthesis or a *nonsensuous* synthesis. This possibility is actualized in religion. Religion differs from art insofar as it is a mediated form of absolute knowledge/spirit, and insofar as it functions on a higher level of mental representations (*Vorstellungen*). To a great extent, the history of religion runs parallel to world history (E3, §562); and art, reaching its zenith in classical civilization (AES2, 127), supplied the springboard for a universal, "absolute" religion (E3, §562), which brought about the divine-human rapprochement that various "determinate" religions, like Zoroastrianism, Judaism, and Greek religion, had only been able to approximate. The perfection of art paved the way for the perfection of religion, in which God would finally reveal himself to humans. Christianity was the religious counterpoint to the largely Hellenic "ethical substance" which was the social cradle of classical art, and to the art-religion that was inseparably connected with classicism (H3, §464; E3, §§557, 563; PS, 491–92).

Christianity, the only explicitly revealed religion (E3, §564), presents a more complex, mediated S/O synthesis than art. It is essentially the mediation of the triune godhead, moving through the moments of universality, particularity, and individuality; creating the world; redeeming it through the son; becoming present in the world through the religious

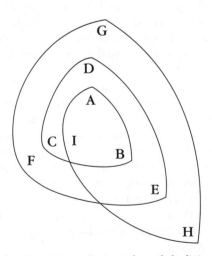

Figure 11. Internal and extrinsic mediations of revealed religion.

community. In greater detail, the mediation of Christianity breaks down in a sub-subdivision of Absolute Spirit into three interlocking "syllogisms" (E3, §571), as shown in Figure 11. The complex, mediated synthesis of subject and object, being and thought, in Christianity—the Absolute Religion—paved the way for the cognitive evolution to absolute knowledge, or philosophy.

Explanation of Figure 11: (1) Moment of universality. The eternal creator (A), replicates himself as his son (B), becoming the Spirit (C) in self-superseding mediation (E3, §567.

(2) Moment of particularity. The triune divinity (D) expresses itself in self-mediation extrinsically (E) through the split between heaven and earth, spirit and nature, leading to (F) the dichotomy between good and evil in the finite human spirit, immersed in nature but relating itself to eternity (E3, §568).

(3) Moment of individuality. The eternal son (G) immerses himself in human existence and suffering to negate the negation, becoming (H) an object of emulation gradually assimilated by his fellow humans, and leading to (I) the incorporation of his spirit into the community of believers (E3, §§569–70.

D. Philosophy

According to Hegel, philosophy as Absolute Knowledge-Spirit is the final unification of the immediate sensuous syntheses of art and the mediated representational syntheses of religion. In philosophy, the sensuous immediacy of art is laid aside, as are the sequential aspects of religious mentations (H3, §472; E3, §§572–73). The result is a mediated *conceptual* coordination of the oppositions of being and thought, in which the immediacy of art is retained, but in a nonsensuous mode.

Philosophy raises the mediations of religion to the highest level in a "system syllogism," or syllogism of syllogisms, which expresses the pure conceptual-ideal interrelationships adumbrated by revealed religion (see Figure 12).

Explanation of Figure 12: (1) First syllogism, L-N-S. Nature as the middle term splits up on one side into its logical essence, and on the other gives rise to the freedom of Spirit (E3, §575.

(2) Second syllogism, N-S-L. Spirit as the middle term presupposes nature and connects nature with its logical aspects (E3, §576).

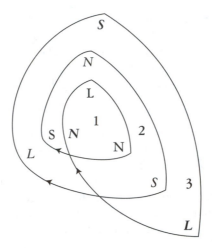

Figure 12. Syllogism of syllogisms.

(3) Third syllogism, *S-L-N*. The Logical Idea on the one hand functions as the culmination of nature and Spirit, and on the other hand constantly sets them in motion and returns them to unity (E3, §577).

In this "syllogism of syllogisms," Logic (L) in the outer circle (syllogism) becomes Absolute Knowledge/Spirit *par excellence,* insofar as the logical Idea is the culminating fusion of subjectivity and objectivity, being and thought, and also mediates dynamically between them.

Hegel's claim (E3, §572, AES1, 143–45, PH, 68–69) is that philosophy is the synthesis of religion, in which subjectivity predominates, and art, in which objectivity predominates. This needs further examination. If we take into account the development of "syllogisms" in religion and philosophy, it is not too difficult to see in what sense he means that philosophy, as it takes over the "mediating" function of revealed religion, raises it to a higher, conceptual level, a higher form of subjectivity, transforming representations and feeling into thought. But it is more difficult to see in what sense the objectivity of *art* is subsumed into philosophy. Thus Hösle finds this claim dubious, on the grounds that there is equivocation between divergent senses of "objectivity" (Hösle 593–94). In what sense does philosophy incorporate the "immediate vision" (E3, §573) of art?

In order to understand this, we have to take into account the nature of the "content" that is given various forms by art, religion and philosophy. According to Hegel, the content in all these cases, is the same—

religious (E3, §554). Art in its paradigmatic sense had to do with the divine: for a devotee in ancient Greece, statues of the gods were not just great works of art but elicited repose in the divine; and audiences at the tragedies of Aeschylus or Sophocles (unlike modern theatergoers) were not just watching a play but were taking part, even as spectators, in a divine drama. Religion proper subsequently brings out this common religious content explicitly; and philosophy raises the same content to a conceptual level (PSK, §§802–03). If we are looking for philosophical content which avoids subject-object dichotomies and best expresses the union of nature and spirit, human and divine, and other oppositions, we cannot fail to notice that the "subject matter" of religion has always been the unity-in-distinction of these oppositions; and, in Hegel's view, Christianity accomplishes this synthesis better (more explicitly) than other religions. Thus speculative philosophy, avoiding all wasteful engagement with noumena or "things in themselves," finds its most appropriate subject matter in the S/O syntheses which religion has already produced.

The sections earlier in this chapter on Hegel's political philosophy and philosophy of history offer examples of the detailed way in which he tried in the domain of "objective Spirit" to "flesh out" the rational/conceptual significance of basic Christian tenets—the "kingdom of God" in his political philosophy and "providence" in his Philosophy of History. As we arrive at "absolute Spirit" in the final Concept of philosophy, it should become especially clear, Hegel says, that:

> God is the starting point and the end of everything; everything has its origin in God, and everything returns to him. God is the one and only object of philosophy: to concentrate on him, to perceive everything in him, to trace everything back to him as well as derive all particulars from him and justify everything just to the extent that it remains in connection with him, lives by his radiance and has his spirit. Thus philosophy is theology; and to be occupied with philosophy—or rather, in philosophy—is intrinsically the service of God.[44]

E. God, Freedom and Immortality: The Reconsideration

Hegel's idea of philosophy thus stands at the antipode of Kant's critique of metaphysics (see pages 71ff above). Kant maintained that there is an unbridgeable rift between truths that can be known through synthetic knowledge and objects of religious faith. The three traditional major concerns of metaphysics—God, freedom, and immortality—are "off limits" to ordinary human understanding (CPR, Bxxx, B7, A798–799

= B826–827). Kant allows that we can have a priori knowledge of freedom as a noumenon, but we can have no "understanding" in the strict sense of that term, since this would require a synthesis of categories with phenomena (CPrR, 6, 50, 57, 354); the postulates of immortality and God are corollaries of our noumenal knowledge of freedom (CPR, B395; CPrR, 3–4). Hegel, considering such "critical" limitations concerning "what we can know" to be examples of faltering timidity (see pages 127–28 above), held not only that religion is accessible to reason, but that philosophy should resolutely *begin* with the insights of religion as content which simply stands in need of the more sophisticated, systematic form that only philosophy can provide. Probably the best way to understand the implications of this bifurcation of Kant's and Hegel's approaches is to consider how Hegel treats God, freedom, and immortality—often very directly rebutting Kant.

God: With regard to the validity of traditional proofs of the existence of God, Hegel contrasts his approach explicitly with Kant's. Kant (CPR, A599=B627) rejects Anselm's "ontological" proof, which (as discussed earlier; see page 60) is that since God is the greatest thing we can conceive of, our concept of God must include real existence (if it did not, there would be a concept of something greater—the same thing, but existing). Kant makes his famous remark that a real hundred dollars does not contain a cent more than the concept of the same hundred dollars, but who would not prefer to have the real hundred dollars? Hegel sees Kant's error as resulting from a very pedestrian idea of the experience of reality:

> The experiencing, the examining, of the world signifies for Kant nothing else but that over here a candlestick is standing and over there a snuffbox. I grant, if what we know is "experience" as a synthesizing of thought and sense-data, certainly the infinite can not be known in the sense that we have a sensory perception of it! But you don't want to demand sensory perception for the verification of the infinite. Spirit exists only for Spirit (HP, 352–53).

Kant's mistake is in assuming a dichotomy between concepts and reality; this assumption is groundless—the dichotomy is artificial. One of the strongest arguments against this assumption is ordinary human experience:

> According to the Kantian notion we are stuck with the difference [between concept and existence]; dualism is the last word. This is the

poor excuse, for what should be absolute and ultimate, that we encounter with Kant (HP3, 361).

The problem with Kant's analogy of a hundred dollars is that he is overly selective, and the example he chose is irrelevant to the issue of the validity of the ontological proof:

> While there is certainly some justification for saying that the concept differs from existence, still the difference of God from the hundred dollars and other finite things is even greater [than the difference of concept from existence]. It is *the definition of finite things* that concept and existence are different in them, that concept and reality, soul and body are separable, that therefore they are transitory and perishable. In contrast, the abstract definition of God is that His concept and His existence are unseparated and inseparable (SL1, 92).

The solution of the Kantian impasse—which is also a partial vindication of Anselm's insight—is to take a lead from Christian revelation and focus on the Idea of God as *Spirit:*

> The standpoint in which we are situated is the Christian view, wherein we have God's concept in its total freedom; this concept is identical with existence. . . . We have to consider existence not in the poverty of abstraction, not in bare immediacy, but existence as the *existence of God,* as the totally *concrete* existence, *distinct* from God himself. . . . The unity [of concept and existence] is to be grasped as *absolute process,* as the life process, of God, such that both aspects are distinct in this unity, but the unity itself is the absolute activity of eternally generating itself (PRe2, 533).

Immortality: Hegel's approach to the question of immortality is partly historical. He finds the first great step toward the idea of personal immortality (as contrasted with the impersonal immortality of Indian religion, and with the vague abstraction of a separate realm of the dead among the ancient Egyptians) in the Greeks' belief in the passage of individuals as "shades" into Hades after death:

> The idea that the spirit is immortal implies that the human individual has in himself an infinite worth. . . . The fact that the spirit is infinite in itself is expressed along with immortality (PH, 266).
>
> [In the Greek idea of the "shade"] there comes forth, although at first just as a weak facsimile, and not yet as the absolute demand of Spirit, the idea of the eternity of the subjective, individual spirit, the idea of *immortality.* . . . Here we find self-consciousness *fulfilled in itself,* spiritual, sub-

jectivity taken up into the universal substance and thus known intrinsically as *Idea* (PRe2, 129).

This foreshadowing becomes a clear, mediated idea through the
influence of the Christian religion, inculcating explicit consciousness of
the infinite worth of the *individual:*

> The withdrawal into innermost self-consciousness [in the Christian reli-
> gion] is the self-awareness that infinitely *divests itself of its particularity and
> the characteristics peculiar to it,* and possesses infinite value just in the love
> that is comprised in, and derived from, infinite anguish. All immediacy
> in which a person had value is cast aside; it is only in *mediation* that such
> value, but now an infinite value, attaches to the person, and that *subjec-
> tivity becomes genuinely infinite* and in-and-for-itself. . . . Herein lies the
> grounding for the fact that the *immortality of the soul* in the Christian reli-
> gion has become a defined doctrine (PRe2, 302–3).

The important thing in the Christian doctrine of immortality, in
Hegel's eyes, is not the promise of life after death or of rewards to be
received in the afterlife, but precisely this emphasis on the infinite worth
of the individual subjectivity. As the philosophical concept of immortality is developed, Hegel tries assiduously to salvage the concept of
immortality implicit in Christianity, while leaving behind all religious
imagery of heaven or continuance in time after death.

Günther Nicolin, in his compilation of anecdotes about Hegel,
includes a story that once, when Hegel's wife asked him what he
thought about the immortality of the soul, Hegel did not say a word,
but simply pointed to their Bible.[45] If this story is true, it would be a
mistake to take it in a Kantian sense, as if Hegel were indicating that we
can have no knowledge of such things but must simply "make room for
faith." Hegel is opposed not only to Kant's assertion that we can have
no trustworthy knowledge of immortality, but also to Kant's substitute
for a "proof," of immortality—namely, the postulate of an endless pursuit of the moral good which relegates immortality to an indefinite
future or "afterlife" (CPrR, 127). For Hegel, immortality is a quality of
Spirit that can be known and begins here and now:

> "Mortal" is what can die; "immortal" is that which can arrive at a state
> where dying can make no entry. [Consider, for comparison,] "flamma-
> ble" and "inflammable"—in this case burning is just a possibility encoun-
> tered extrinsically by an object. The determination of existence, however,
> is not such an extrinsic possibility, but a positively determined quality,
> which the existent already has within itself. In like fashion, the "immor-

tality of the soul" should not be construed as if it first entered into actuality "later on"; immortality is a present quality. Spirit is eternal, and consequently present already; Spirit in its freedom exists within the domain of the limited. For Spirit as thinking, as pure knowledge, the object is the universal; the universal is eternity, which is not mere duration, in the sense that the mountains have duration, but *knowledge*. The eternity of Spirit is brought into consciousness in this knowledge, in this separation from involvement with the natural, the contingent, the extrinsic—a separation which has attained to the infinity of existence-for-self. (PRe2, 260–61).

Hegel's approach to the "problem of immortality" is reminiscent of Aristotle's concept of "present immortality" in his *Nicomachean Ethics,* where he admonishes us to "strain every nerve" to make ourselves immortal.[46] But Hegel portrays our "present immortality" as something already attained, and as something about which we have greater certainty than Aristotle and the ancient Greeks because of the necessary connection of immortality with the Idea of infinite personhood distilled from Christianity.

Freedom: Kant set the stage for the modern "freedom problem" in his Third Antinomy (CPR, A444–B472ff), where he gives two contradictory "proofs": that there exists and there does not exist a "free" causality over and above ordinary phenomenal chains of causal determinations. Escaping from this hopeless theoretical contradiction, Kant—on practical, moral grounds—posited freedom as an a priori noumenal causality. In Kant's system, freedom as a noumenon seems to be the main pillar supporting the distinctions fundamental to the system: subject versus object, and phenomenon versus noumenon. Hegel applauds Kant for indicating with his antinomies that every reality implies the coexistence of opposites (freedom and determinism are an example), but he faults Kant for not taking the next logical step to grasp the union of the opposites in question—ordinary causality and "free" causality, necessity and freedom:

> A freedom that contained no necessity, a pure necessity without freedom—these are abstract and unauthentic determinations. . . . When reference is made to "necessity" one commonly interprets the necessity immediately as extrinsic determination, as, for instance, in finite mechanics, a body only is moved if it is pushed by another body. . . . This is mere external necessity, not the genuine inner necessity; for the inner necessity is freedom (E1, §35, Zusatz).
>
> If we take a closer look at the [Kantian] antinomy of freedom and necessity, it turns out that what the Understanding interprets as "free-

dom" and "necessity" are actually just ideal moments of the true freedom and the true necessity [of the Concept], and that no truth attaches to these two moments in the state of separation (E1, §48, Zusatz).

The application of the concept of absolute will or absolute freedom to the political realm has already been discussed above (page 129). As we saw, the keynote of Hegel's theory of the state is not precisely the institutionalization of freedom but the development of a constitution which will make freedom a necessity, or will at least make it difficult not to be free. In his course in 1810 on "ethical theory for the underclass," Hegel also applied the concept of the union of freedom and necessity to the moral realm:

> Human freedom from natural drives does not consist in *not having any drives* and escaping from one's nature; it consists rather in recognizing nature in general as a necessity and therewith as something rational, and perfecting it in tandem with its will. In this way a person finds himself subject to force only to the extent that he carries out contingent and capricious deviations and designs in opposition to the universal.[47]

In his aesthetics, Hegel gives an illustration of how a similar conjunction of opposites applies in the relationship between melody and harmony in music:

> Bona fide freedom does not stand over against necessity as against something foreign and hence oppressive and oppressing. Rather, freedom [in melody] holds to this substantiality of necessity [in harmony] as something that dwells within freedom itself, as an essence identical with freedom; following the demands of necessity, freedom is thus just obeying its own laws, and conforming to its own nature, so that in any departure from what has been laid down it would be turning away from itself and untrue to itself (AES3, 187).

Absolute Knowledge/Spirit in Hegel's later system manifests itself in areas in which there is a transparent fusion of being and thought: in art, which exists not just as an "art object" but as a source of religious transcendence; in religion, which does not consist only of imaginative projections or myths but is a means of coming into contact with being itself and experiencing firsthand the mediated synthesis of being and thought; and in philosophy, which enters conceptually into the mediation of being and thought, bringing these mediations into conclusions which in their intuitive clarity are comparable to the immediate syntheses of classical art. Examples of philosophical coordinations of being and thought are to be found in the Idea of God not just as a transcendent object or immanent subjectivity, but as infinite Spirit manifesting itself in human consciousness; in the Idea of immortality as a real property of thought itself, whether in the present life or in some future life; and in the Idea of freedom not as a power distinct from necessity but as deriving from and depending on the necessities which it coordinates and channels.

It goes without saying that such coordinations result in paradoxes. Freedom requires close collaboration with necessities; immortality is present in this life and is cognizable with certainty; God is not an object to be known but a subject-object acquiring self-consciousness within humans. Oppositions which are abandoned as metaphysical impasses by Kant are thus reinterpreted by Hegel as catalysts for advances in speculative philosophy.

Chapter Seven

What Is Living and
What Is Dead in Hegel Today?

First of all, I should perhaps apologize for purloining the title of a book by Benedetto Croce (1907)[1] and affixing it to my much more modest effort in this final chapter. However, the addition of "today" will serve to differentiate the present chapter from Croce's book and, at the same time, to give an indication of the affinity between the two: an updating and a critical reassessment of Hegel and Hegelianism.

In his book on Hegel, Croce came to the conclusion that the weak point in Hegel's system was Hegel's "panlogism"—that "excrescence of Hegel's System" (Croce 192) through which the dualism of Nature and Spirit was smothered; or, to say the same thing in a different way, the unjustified and unjustifiable passage from one distinct and irreducible reality, the "Idea," to another distinct and irreducible reality, Nature. Croce also defended Hegel, however, and thought that Hegel's most important contribution was, in contrast to Bergson and others who would like to renounce thought for intuition, "to have shown that the demand of concrete knowledge is satisfied in the form of thought" (Croce, 214). Croce also indulged in a psychoanalytic speculation that Hegel's nineteenth-century adversaries—Schopenhauer, Janet, and others—hated him because they saw him as the symbol of philosophy itself, "which is without heart and without compassion for the feeble-minded and for the lazy: Philosophy, which is not to be placated with the specious offerings of sentiment and of fancy, nor with the light foods of half-science."

Whatever his strong and weak points, Hegel's appeal has apparently not diminished in our present era, and in fact there are signs of a "Hegel renaissance." A phenomenon that would lead us to believe such a renaissance is in progress is the constant increase of books on Hegel in the last four decades.[2] What are the reasons for this continually growing interest in Hegel? One obvious reason is pragmatic: the necessity for understanding Hegel in order to assess Kierkegaard's reaction against him, Marx's and Sartre's use of Hegelian concepts in developing their own positions, Heidegger's interpretation of Hegel, and Derrida's attack on Hegelian "ontotheology." A second reason is that in some quarters, interest in Hegel is concomitant with a reaction against analytic philosophy.[3] A third reason, however, is that elsewhere this renaissance may be an out-growth of analytic philosophy itself. Richard Bernstein broaches this third possibility, arguing that analytical philosophers are finding more and more that single and discrete analyses "spill over to other issues" (as happens in Hegel's analyses), that progress on epistemological issues requires confrontation with metaphysical issues (a requirement Hegel insisted on), that one can't deal effectively with reference and denotation without getting into ontology (another Hegelian insight), and so forth.[4] A fourth reason, also noted by Bernstein, has to do with developments in philosophy of science that seem to reflect Hegelian themes—e.g., theo-ries about the evolution of scientific paradigms and recognition of the influence of social contexts on scientific theories (Bernstein, 39). A fifth reason has to do with Hegel's political theory: in 1989, renewed interest in this aspect of his work was generated when Francis Fukuyama pub-lished an article in *The National Interest,* portraying Hegel as a prophet of the triumph of liberalism over communism.

All in all, there is much that is living (or that deserves to be revived) in Hegel's system; but the following factors seem to me most significant:

I. Perennial Philosophy

Whether or not philosophy itself is perennial, the idea of a perennial philosophy—espoused by thinkers as diverse as Leibniz and Peirce, and revived by Mortimer Adler and his associates—certainly seems to be perennial. A few decades ago, Adler looked to scholastic realism as an anchor of sanity in a philosophical world gone adrift in sectarian rivalry and undisciplined individualism. But the synthesizing power of the great scholastic edifice has proven not to be unlimited. For those still seeking a perennial philosophy but disenchanted with the scholastic model, Hegel may seem an improvement, if not the ultimate answer. For Hegel saw all philosophical schools and systems as the unfolding of one central problematic—the relationship of being to thought—and he also managed to synthesize the "transcendental turn" (Kant's "Coperni-can revolution") into his overall schema (something scholastic realism was constitutionally unable to accomplish). The synthesizing power of the Hegelian system is of course challenged to the utmost in an intellec-tual world grown accustomed to evolution, relativity, the demise of monarchical political systems, the decline of the west, and multivalued logics. But Hegel's general thesis, that philosophy in all its forms and stages has been concerned with working out the relationship of being to thought, may be worth serious reconsideration.

II. History of Philosophy

Perhaps a more important rallying point of current interest in Hegel is a resurgence of interest in the history of philosophy as an essential—and essentially *philosophical*—pursuit. This renewed interest in history may quite conceivably have been brought about by the very pluralism and factionalism of contemporary philosophy, much as a society in times of confusion or anarchy may grope for stability by studying its own history and heritage. Those who seek in the history of philosophy some illumination about contemporary philosophical goings-on will find a kindred spirit in G. W. F. Hegel; for Hegel, perhaps more than any other modern philosopher, emphasized the history of philosophy, and in a very real sense even identified philosophy with its history.

III. Generalism

I mentioned above that in Croce's estimation Hegel was, to many of his antiphilosophical or anti-intellectual enemies, a symbol of philosophy. In our own time, yet another reason why many people are *attracted* to Hegel may be that they see him as a symbol of philosophy—or, more specifically, of that old-style philosophy which openly and unabashedly announced its concern with "knowing all things" in some sort of ultimate way.

Nowadays, anyone who has philosophical inclinations of this sort is best advised to keep silent about them. After all, philosophy, following the example of science, has become extremely specialized and compartmentalized, and in these days of a never-ending "knowledge explosion," who would seriously lay claim to knowing "all things"—the whole universe or even its infinite "areas of discourse"? But for one disgruntled underground species of philosophers, those who can't quite give up that grandiose aspiration, the study of Hegel allows them to do something of this sort, with a certain degree of respectability and without having to put on airs of being geniuses. However, to fend off charges of Hegelian gnosticism, I should reemphasize that Hegel himself did not claim to "know all things"; he claimed only to have uncovered the "absolute standpoint" making possible a balanced, no longer one-sided perspective, on perennial philosophical issues. This was brought out especially in Chapter 6, in the section on "Absolute Knowledge and Spirit."

IV. Metaphilosophy

The most serious and most important inducement to study Hegel, in my opinion, is an interest in, and a need for, *metaphilosophy.* In the contemporary world, the term "metaphilosophy" has four distinguishable connotations: (1) study of the nature of philosophy; or (2) comparison of one philosophical school with another with regard to various perspectives or points of doctrine; or (3) determining structural interrelationships among various philosophical positions and schools, so that they can be comprehended as a totality; or (4) study of philosophical discourse. (For those who understand "metaphilosphy" in the fourth sense—as a study of philosophical discourse—it becomes the study of *philosophical* discourse about "philosophical discourse.")

Hegel seems relevant to metaphilosophy especially in the first and third senses of the term. As regards the first sense, Hegel was acutely aware that "buck-passing" must stop with philosophy: that if philosophy does not become self-consciously aware of its own methodology and presuppositions, it can depend on no other higher discipline to inculcate such self-consciousness. In Hegel's estimation, it is precisely the critical self-consciousness of the philosopher that supplies a dialectical impetus away from provincial, incomplete, or one-sided positions toward "Absolute Knowledge." As regards the third sense of "metaphilosophy," one of Hegel's most persistent endeavors was to develop a comprehensive "system" of philosophy in which all the various schools of thought—empiricism and idealism, materialism and rationalism, and Platonism, Cartesianism, Kantianism, etc.—could be seen in their proper perspective and interrelationships. Needless to say, Hegel was an incorrigible optimist about the possibility of finding a place for even the strangest bedfellows; and in our day—as we make our way through the intellectual wilds of ethical noncognitivism, process philosophy and its finite God, existential Marxism, second- and third-order linguistic analysts, hermeneuticism, structuralism, and deconstructionism—we could no doubt use a good dose of Hegel's optimism about the possibility of synthesis.

V. Interdisciplinary Integration

One salutary result of the study of Hegel has been a holistic view. One cannot read Hegel seriously and sympathetically without beginning to view the specialization and prima facie autonomy of various branches of philosophy as unnecessary (ontologically or otherwise) and even counterproductive. To Hegel's mind, metaphysics must be studied in conjunction with epistemology and logic; ethics in conjunction with politics, philosophical anthropology, and law; and so forth. We do not necessarily have to agree with Hegel that a holistic approach is the only viable approach; but we would no doubt benefit from complementing the process of specialization with a process of integration, analysis with synthesis.

VI. Political Representation Theory

One result of the study of Hegel's political philosophy has been a critical reassessment of democratic ideology. Hegel was in harmony with liberal democratic theory in his emphasis on participation by citizens in government; but he was sharply at odds with the democratic theorists regarding the mode of such participation. As mentioned earlier (page 118), Hegel had no patience with the idea that the formula "one man, one vote" would guarantee political self-determination. He insisted that the "input" of the citizenry should be mediated by natural groupings (for example, labor unions as well as industrial interests), and that government should be highly structured to ensure that all the various natural or organic groupings in a state would find a place in its national assemblies. At a time when Hitler's election on the basis of the "one man, one vote" is still a fairly recent memory—and when "control" over the federal government by average American working people is often reduced to perilous choices, every few years, between congressional or presidential candidates neither of whom is thought satisfactory—it would be appropriate for us to ask, like Hegel, whether there is any more natural way to ensure constant participation by and representation of citizens in a free state. Especially with today's revolutionary advances in communication technologies, the possibilities of full democratic participation have to be rethought.

VII. Paradox

The prevalence and centrality of paradox in Hegel's system was discussed in Chapter 1. To most western philosophers, of course, paradox is something found exclusively in poetry, eastern philosophy and the Christian gospels; a paradox in philosophy is something to be avoided—perhaps studied but certainly not intentionally cultivated. We have seen that Hegel's philosophy, in contrast, is replete with paradoxes, systematically produced and not infrequently proffered as a kind of *solution* rather than as a problem or puzzle.

The existence of paradoxes puts to the test our linguistic and logical conventions regarding univocity and noncontradiction, but we should not dismiss them simply on this ground. Dismissing paradox for such a reason would be analogous to, say, Einstein's dismissing the change of mass of subatomic particles at high speeds because it flouted Newtonian physics. It was by going beyond this apparent contradiction that Einstein arrived at new paradoxical insights; analogously, it may just so happen that some philosophical truths are apparent contradictions on the level of ordinary logic, but paradoxical truths nevertheless. When we think of the consensus among physicists, biologists, and chemists on many foundational issues and, by contrast, the lack of consensus—and the many contradictions—among philosophers on every issue, it may not seem unlikely that paradox, which incorporates oppositions and contradictions but also surpasses them, may be the most appropriate mode of expression in philosophy. In other words, traditional questions—such as "Is essence prior to existence?" "How do you derive 'ought' from 'is'?" "Is beauty in the eye of the beholder?" "Why is there something rather than nothing?" and "How do we know the existence of other minds?"—may be unsusceptible of satisfactory answers in ordinary propositional form, so that we can respond appropriately to them only with paradox.

VIII. Christian Philosophy

I would like to suggest that one final important aspect of Hegel's philosophy is that it is a Christian philosophy. One must be careful in using the term "Christian philosophy," since it seems reminiscent of scholasticism or Thomism, which several decades ago was an object of disdain by "mainstream" philosophers, who accused it of being partially apologetics and partly theology. Hegel's philosophy is not an apologetic, but it is thoroughly theological, as Hegel himself asserts in places (see, e.g., page 137). Hegel's theology is speculative and patristic, rather than biblical or "systematic" in the current theological sense; but it offers intensive examination of many important theological issues. Karl Barth suggests in one place that Hegel is the Thomas Aquinas of Protestantism;[5] and the Catholic theologian Hans Küng devotes a book to a constructive elaboration of Hegel's Christology.[6] But the conflict between leftist and rightist interpretations of Hegel, begun after his death, is still going strong. Thus Robert Solomon, in a book on Hegel, argues at length that Hegel, in spite of his protests to the contrary, was an atheist or at least a pantheist;[7] and H. S. Harris suggests that Hegel's description of his Philosophy of History as a "theodicy" was a ploy to distract attention from the revolutionary social theory of the *Phenomenology* (Harris 1983, 87). But any attempt to construe Hegel's philosophy as "closet atheism" or "closet pantheism" would need to explain away literally thousands of references affirming Protestant Christianity.

It is true that, because of his confidence in the power of Reason to incorporate and supersede the doctrines of faith, Hegel seems in places to tend toward a sort of gnosticism. But one must understand that Hegel took Anselm's dictum *fides quaerens intellectum* (faith seeking understanding) even more seriously than Anselm himself did. It would never have occurred to Anselm, for example, to actually try through "reason" to present in a philosophy of history an apologetic for the presence of God in the world, a justification of the way that divine providence is leading humankind to freedom.

It is not only leftist Hegelians who fail to appreciate such efforts, but also rightist Hegelians and many Christian philosophers, such as Eric Voegelin and Karl Löwith, for whom the fact that Hegel's God is a *worldly* God is a scandal. Without doubt, it is only the middle group of philosophers, who *can* believe in a God of this sort, who will find in Hegel a viable paradigm of Christian philosophy.

IX. Problems with Hegel

Let me now balance this account of the positive aspects of Hegelianism with an appraisal of some of Hegel's more salient deficiencies and errors.

Many critics of Hegel, including Marx and Kierkegaard, have pointed out that his "system" was a magnificent failure, though they flattered Hegel by extensive imitation. Marx tried to use Hegel's dialectical methodology without succumbing to Hegel's ontology; Kierkegaard in his "aesthetic" works reinterprets or reapplies many ideas from Hegel's phenomenology.[8] Others exonerate Hegel's system but consider his dialectic the drawback.[9] I side with the former group. Hegel's system is obviously patterned after Fichte's and Schelling's attempts to build systems and is thus "dated." Although Hegel's system provides a wealth of insights, it would not be worthwhile to follow in his footsteps by philosophizing in sets of intertwining and nested triads. However, alternative systems are conceivable; and in any case, there seems to be something instinctive, for humans, about building systems. Kierkegaard, for instance, could never have been an effective antagonist to Hegel without his own countersystem.

Again, not to pass over the shadows for the light, I should mention that Hegel, influenced by his own cultural milieu, also had some very deep-seated prejudices. For one thing, in line with the Hellenist sentiment of his era, he idolized the Greeks, but he saw fit to characterize the Romans—of the republic and the empire—as essentially a band of robbers who got together and then required strong, practical laws and eventually tyranny to keep them from turning on each other (PH, 344ff, 512). And although one could interpret parts of Hegel's chapter on "Faith and Insight" in the *Phenomenology of Spirit* as a defense of the Catholic veneration of relics, crucifixes, and the host, nevertheless when Hegel speaks explicitly in his *Lectures on the Philosophy of History* and *Lectures on the Philosophy of Religion* about Catholicism, he frequently refers to it, with extreme Lutheran bias, as an example of superstition and brainwashing, and as a major obstacle to human freedom in the modern world.

Hegel's historical and geographical provinciality likewise seems remarkable, if we consider that he was the great exponent of a universal "Absolute Spirit." In the *Philosophy of History,* Hegel not only "writes off" China as being outside history but refuses to give any serious attention to Russia or the other Slavic countries because they contributed nothing important to (European) history. And even Hegel's empathy with western European nations was severely limited, as is shown by his disagreement with Kant about the possibility of anything like a league of nations (PR, §333, Zusatz).

Hegel, like Kant,[10] seemed to think of Negroes as a definitely inferior race. He theorized that although they were stronger and more educable than American Indians (PH, 109), Negroes represented the inharmonious state of "natural man," before humans' attainment of consciousness of God and their own individuality (PH, 123); and that, in general, white skin was the most perfect harbinger of both physical health and conscious receptivity![11] In line with these sentiments, he of course eliminated the whole continent of Africa from explicit historical consideration, except insofar as certain Africans were influenced by European Mediterranean culture. He offered a left-handed compliment to "the Negroes," in that he ascribed natural talent to them, whereas the American Indians, he opined, had no such natural endowments (PH, 82).

Hegel's ideas of women similarly reflect "scientific" attitudes that prevailed at the time but would now be considered sexist. For example, in his treatment of the family in the *Philosophy of Right,* he generalizes that women are ruled by feeling, can be educated only by something like osmosis, and should never be put in charge of a state (PR, §166, Zusatz).

Hegel's praise of war and overall militarism (see, e.g., PR, §324 and Zusatz), even though it was tempered by his opposition to nationalism (Hösle 582n), strongly influenced nineteenth- and twentieth-century war ideologies, up to and including Nazism (Hösle 581). Actually, such sentiments are surprising, coming from Hegel, if we take into account the importance of sublimation (*Aufhebung*) in his philosophy. If, for example, the "life and death struggle" (PSK, §187) is "sublimated" (*aufgehoben*) into a master-slave relationship, and if that relationship in its turn is sublimated into Stoicism, etc.—why cannot the propensity to war itself be sublimated into some higher form of resolving conflict?

Still, as we assess Hegel's evaluations in hindsight, we have to keep in mind his admonition that philosophers are a product of their time and cannot rise above it (PR, Preface, 26). This is certainly true in his own case; but it is worth noting that he has been unique in seeing this time-boundedness to be an insuperable limitation on a philosopher's prophetic capabilities.

I would like to conclude by asking the question Benedetto Croce posed at the end of his book: Should we be Hegelians today? Like Croce, I would answer, "yes and no". No, because the sorts of deficiencies I have just mentioned are a formidable obstacle to presenting Hegel's philosophy as the philosophy for our times. I am sure that Hegel himself, who insisted strongly on the historical and cultural limitations of any philosophy, would not be a Hegelian now— if by "Hegelian" is meant someone who champions monarchy, systems built out of triads, outdated scientific ideas, and so forth. But, yes, we should be Hegelians if by "Hegelian" is meant, for example, someone who gives explicit attention to dialectical oppositions in the sciences and in the contemporary spirit and tries to bridge these oppositions on a philosophical level; who tries to bring the fragmented specializations in philosophy into some type of systematic unity; who sees the subject-object relationship as a fundamental philosophical problematic worthy of serious attention and hard work; who is interested in fashioning a new rapprochement between faith and knowledge; and who is concerned with ensuring meaningful and effective participation by citizens in their government.

Notes and References

Preface

1. G. W. F. Hegel, *Werke* (*Works*), E. Moldenhauer and K. M. Michel, eds. (Frankfurt am Main: Suhrkamp Verlag, 1969-1971), vol. 2, 582.

2. There is some debate as to whether Hegel actually took part in this demonstration. H. S. Harris in *Hegel's Development: Towards the Sunlight, 1770-1801* (Oxford: Clarendon, 1972): 63, 115n, characterizes the story as part of the "Hegel myth"; but Franz Wiedmann in *Hegel: An Illustrated Biography*, J. Neugroschel, trans. (New York: Pegasus, 1968): 20-21, and Horst Althaus, *Hegel und die heroischen Jahre der Philosophie: Eine Biographie* (Freiburg: Carl Hanser Verlag, 1992), 40, cite it as authentic. These works by Wiedmann and Althaus are hereafter cited in text.

3. See Herman Nohl, *Hegels theologische Jugendschriften*, Tübingen, 1907, 345-51.

Chapter One

1. G. W. F. Hegel, *Enzyklopädie der philosophischen Wissenschaften* (*Encyclopedia of Philosophical Sciences*) 1st (Heidelberg) edition, Hermann Glockner, ed. (Stuttgart: Friedrich Frommann Verlag, 1968), §15. The three parts of this *Encyclopedia*—Logic, Philosophy of Nature, and Philosophy of Spirit—are hereafter cited in text as H1, H2, and H3. Note that, for the reader's convenience, all abbreviations are listed in the frontispiece (see page xxi).

2. G. W. F. Hegel, *Wissenschaft der Logik* (*Science of Logic*), in *Werke*, E. Moldenhauer and K. M. Michel, eds. (Frankfurt am Main: Suhrkamp Verlag, 1969-1971), vols. 5-6; vol. 5, 52. Vol. 5 is hereafter cited in text as SL1; vol. 6 as SL2.

3. G. W. F. Hegel, *Enzyklopädie der philosophischen Wissenschaften* (*Encyclopedia of Philosophical Sciences*), in *Werke*, E. Moldenhauer and K. M. Michel, eds. (Frankfurt am Main: Suhrkamp Verlag, 1969-1971), vols. 8-10; vol. 8, §162. Vol. 8 is hereafter cited in text as E1; vol. 9 as E2; and vol. 10 as E3.

4. G. W. F. Hegel, *Phänomenologie des Geistes* (*Phenomenology of Spirit*), Hans-Friedrich Wessels and Heinrich Clairmont, eds. (Hamburg: Felix Meiner Verlag, 1988), 27. Hereafter cited in text as PS.

5. Richard Rorty, *Philosophy and the Mirror of Nature* (Oxford: Blackwell, 1980).

6. G. W. F. Hegel, *Vorlesungen über die Geschichte der Philosophie* (*Lectures on the History of Philosophy*), *Werke*, E. Moldenhauer and K. M. Michel, eds. (Frankfurt am Main: Suhrkamp Verlag, 1969-1971), vols. 18-20; vol. 20, 446.

Vol. 18 (history of ancient philosophy) is hereafter cited in text as HP1; vol. 19 (transition to medieval philosophy) as HP2; and vol. 20 (history of modern philosophy) as HP3.

7. See H. Kainz, *Hegel's* Phenomenology, *Part I: Analysis and Commentary* (Tuscaloosa: University of Alabama Press, 1976), 13-14.

8. G. W. F. Hegel, *Differenz des Fichteschen und Schellingschen Systems der Philosophie (The Difference between Schelling's and Fichte's System of Philosophy), Werke,* E. Moldenhauer and K. M. Michel, eds. (Frankfurt am Main: Suhrkamp Verlag, 1969-1971), vols. 1-20; vol. 2, 122. Hereafter cited in text as DFS.

9. Donald Verene, *Hegel's Recollection* (Albany, New York: State University of New York Press, 1985), 19.

10. Fragment 5, Hermann Diels's arrangement.

Chapter Two

1. Otto Pöggeler, *Hegels Idee einer Phänomenologie des Geistes* (Freiburg-München: Karl Abler Verlag, 1973), 200-201. Hereafter cited in text.

2. G. W. F. Hegel, *The Berlin Phenomenology,* M. J. Petry, ed. and trans. (Dordrecht: Reidel, 1981), xvii-xviii. With reference to the parts of the Jena phenomenology dealing with nature, see also M. J. Petry, ed., *Hegel's Philosophy of Nature* (New York: Humanities, 1970), vol. I, 83, 85. Hereafter cited in text as E2P.

3. G. W. F. Hegel, *Hegel's Phenomenology of Spirit: Translated and Annotated by Howard P. Kainz* (University Park: Pennsylvania State University Press, 1994), §§242-43. Hereafter cited in text as PSK.

4. Wolfgang Bonsiepen, "Phänomenologie des Geistes," in Otto Pöggeler, *Hegel* (Freiburg-München: Karl Alber Verlag, 1977), 74. Hereafter cited in text.

5. Vittorio Hösle, *Hegels System: Der Idealismus der Subjektivität und das Problem der Intersubjektivität* (Hamburg: Felix Meiner Verlag, 1988), 386-88. Hereafter cited in text.

Chapter Three

1. Denise Souche-Dagues, *Le cercle hégélien* (Paris: Presses Universitaires de France, 1986), 17.

2. Robert Grant McRae, *Philosophy and the Absolute* (The Hague: Nijhoff, 1985), 31f, 41.

Chapter Four

1. Georgia Apostolopoulou, "Probleme der neugriechischen Hegel-Übersetzung," in *Übersetzen, Verstehen, Brücken Bauen* (Berlin: Erich Schmidt Verlag, 1993), Teil 1, 242-43.

2. Immanuel Kant, *Critique of Judgment,* §77.

3. *Glauben und Wissen . . . (Faith and Knowledge . . .)* in *Werke,* E. Moldenhauer and K. M. Michel, eds. (Frankfurt am Main: Suhrkamp Verlag, 1969-1971), vols. 1-20; vol. 2, 327-28.

4. Plato, *Republic* vi, 508b-509b.

5. F. W. J. Schelling, "Darstellung meines Systems der Philosophie," in *Schellings Werke,* M. Schröter, Ed. (München: Beck und Oldenbourg, 1927), Vol 3, §1.

6. Immanuel Kant, *Critique of Pure Reason,* A407 to B433-34. Hereafter cited in text as K-CPR.

7. Howard Kainz, *Paradox, Dialectic and System: A Contemporary Reconstruction of the Hegelian Problematic* (University Park: Pennsylvania State University Press, 1988). Hereafter cited in text.

8. G. W. F. Hegel, *The Philosophy of Right,* in *Werke,* E. Moldenhauer and K. M. Michel, eds. (Frankfurt am Main: Suhrkamp Verlag, 1969-1971), vols. 1-20; vol. 7, 24. Hereafter cited in text as PR.

Chapter Five

1. Philip Wheelwright, ed., *The Presocratics* (New York: Odyssey, 1966), 98. Hereafter cited in text.

2. Hegel, *Lectures on the History of Philosophy: The Lectures of 1825-1826,* vol. 3, *Medieval and Modern Philosophy,* Robert F. Brown, ed.; R. F. Brown and J. M. Stewart with the assistance of H. S. Harris, trans., 28. Hereafter cited in text as HP3BS.

Chapter Six

1. Aristotle, *Physics,* Richard McKeon, ed.; Hardie and Gaye, trans., *Basic Works of Aristotle* (New York: Random House, 1941), vol. I, 9, 192a, 34ff.. Hereafter cited as A-PHYS.

2. Aristotle, *Metaphysics,* Richard McKeon, ed.; W. D. Ross, trans., *Basic Works of Aristotle* (New York: Random House, 1941), vol. VI, 1, 1026a, 15-33. Hereafter cited in text as A-MET.

3. Aristotle, *De Caelo,* Richard McKeon, ed.; J. L. Stocks, trans., *Basic Works of Aristotle* (New York: Random House, 1941), vol. I, 9, 279a, 12-23; A-PHYS VIII, 10, 267b, 6-7.

4. A-MET XII, 3, 25-28; Aristotle, *De Anima,* Richard McKeon, ed.; J. A. Smith trans., *Basic Works of Aristotle* (New York: Random House, 1941), III, 5. Hereafter cited in text as A-DeA.

5. Immanuel Kant, *Fundamental Principles of a Metaphysic of Morals,* T. K. Abbot, trans. (Indianapolis: Bobbs-Merrill, 1949), 37. Hereafter cited in text as K-FPMM.

6. Stephen Körner, *Kant* (Baltimore: Penguin Books, 1955), 78.

7. Norman Kemp Smith, *A Commentary on Kant's "Critique of Pure Reason"* (New York: Humanities, 1962), 33. Hereafter cited in text.

8. Eckhart Förster, "Kants Metaphysikbegriff: Vor-kritisch, kritisch, nach-kritisch," in *Metaphysik nach Kant?* Dieter Henrich und Rolf-Peter Horstmann (Stuttgart: Klett-Cotta, 1988).

9. Arthur Schopenhauer, *The World as Will and Representation,* E. Payne, trans. (Indian Hills, Colorado: Falcon's Wing, 1958), vol. I, 470-71.

10.   The external impetus from the side of the non-ego, which Fichte (in Hegel's interpretation) presupposed as a kind of content for an ego caught up in a subjectivist extreme.

11.   See Chapter 4, page 41.

12.   See, e.g., Leslie Armour, *Logic and Reality: An Investigation into the Idea of a Dialectical System* (Assen: Van Gorcum, 1972); George Melhuish, *The Paradoxical Nature of Reality* (Bristol: St. Vincent's Press, 1973); and Eric Toms, *Being, Negation and Logic* (Oxford: Basil Blackwell, 1962). I have indicated a possible way in which a speculative-dialectical metaphysical system might be generated in Kainz 1988, 44-48.

13.   For a comprehensive list of scientific works familiar to Hegel, see E2P 128-41.

14.   Dieter Wandschneider, *Raum, Zeit, Relativität: Grundbestimmungen der Physik in der Perspecktive der Hegelschen Naturphilosophie* (Frankfurt am Main: Vittorio Klostermann, 1982), 33. Hereafter cited in text.

15.   H. S. Harris, "The Hegel Renaissance in the Anglo-Saxon World Since 1945," *The Owl of Minverva*, vol. 15, 1 (Fall 1983), 95. Hereafter cited in text.

16.   Karl Popper, *Conjectures and Refutations: The Growth of Scientific Knowledge* (New York: Basic, 1963), 36-37.

17.   Werner Heisenberg, *Physics and Philosophy* (New York: Harper, 1958), 53, 81. Hereafter cited in text.

18.   "On Formally Undecidable Propositions of *Principia Mathematica* and Related Systems I," Jean van Heijencort, trans., in S. G. Shanker, ed., *Gödel's Theorem* (London and New York: Routledge, 1988).

19.   J. N. Findlay, "Goedelian Sentences: A Non-Numerical Approach," *Mind*, vol. 51 (1952).

20.   G. W. F. Hegel, *Über die wissenshaftlichen Behandlungsarten des Naturrechts . . . (On the Treatment of Natural Law)* in *Werke*, E. Moldenhauer and K. M. Michel, eds. (Frankfurt am Main: Suhrkamp Verlag, 1969-1971), vols. 1-20; vol. 2.

21.   See M. J. Petry's partial bibliography of early-nineteenth-century works on anthropology in his *Hegel's Philosophy of Subjective Spirit* (Dordrecht: Reidel, 1978), vol. 1, lxiii-lxvi. Hereafter cited in text as E3P.

22.   Petry lists Hegel's main sources in E3P xcviii-civ.

23.   See John Barrow and Frank Tipler, *The Anthropic Cosmological Principle* (New York: Oxford University Press, 1986), 127-37.

24.   G. W. F. Hegel, *Vorlesungen über die Philosophie der Geschichte* (*Lectures on the Philosophy of History*), in *Werke*, E. Moldenhauer and K. M. Michel, eds. (Frankfurt am Main: Suhrkamp Verlag, 1969-1971), vol. 12, 512. Hereafter cited in text as PH.

25.   William H. Sheldon, *The Varieties of Temperament* (New York: Harper, 1942), 4.

26.   Thomas Aquinas, *Summa theologiae* (Madrid: Biblioteca de Autores Cristianos, 1961), vol. I, q. 78, a. 3. Hereafter cited in text.

27.   Jacques Barzun, "Is Democratic Theory for Export?" *Society,* vol. 26, 3 (March-April 1989).

28.   See also G. W. F. Hegel, *Philosophie der Religion* in *Werke,* E. Moldenhauer and K. M. Michel, eds. (Frankfurt am Main: Suhrkamp Verlag, 1969-1971), vols. 1-20; vol. 16, 241-44; cited hereafter in text as PRe1.

29.   E3 356-7; and G. W. F. Hegel, *Philosophie der Religion* in *Werke,* E. Moldenhauer and K. M. Michel, eds. (Frankfurt am Main: Suhrkamp Verlag, 1969-1971), vols. 1-20, vol. 17, 331; cited hereafter in text as PRe2.

30.   See also Paul Lakeland, *The Politics of Salvation* (Albany: State University of New York Press, 1984), 91.

31.   See Michael Theunissen, *Hegels Lehre vom absoluten Geist als theologishpolitisher Traktat* (Berlin: de Gruyter, 1970), 372-73.

32.   See Klaus Hartmann, *Die Marxistische Theorie: Eine philosophische Untersuchung zu der Hauptschriften* (Berlin: de Gruyter, 1970), 62; cited hereafter in text.

33.   Compare Augustine, *The City of God,* vol. XX, 9.

34.   G. W. F. Hegel, *Vorlesungen: Ausgewählte Nachschriften und Manuskripte,* vol. 5, *Vorlesungen über die Philosophie der Religion,* Part 3, "Die vollendete Religion," Walter Jaeschke, ed. (Hamburg: Felix Meiner, 1984), 87.

35.   Karl Löwith, *Meaning in History* (Chicago: University of Chicago Press, 1949), 60 ff.

36.   Immanuel Kant, *On History,* L. W. Beck, R. E. Anchor, and E. L. Fackenheim, trans. (New York: Bobbs Merrill, 1963), 147-48, 153.

37.   Pierre Teilhard de Chardin, *The Divine Milieu* (New York: Harper), 133.

38.   M. Scott Peck, *The Road Less Travelled* (New York: Simon & Schuster, 1978), 267.

39.   As mentioned above, in Hegel's technical usage, the philosophical "Concept" is a subjective-objective unity, which goes beyond the figurative representations of religion even though it builds on them.

40.   G. W. F. Hegel, *Vorlesungen: Ausgewählte Nachschriften und Manuskripte,* vol. 3, *Vorlesungen über die Philosophie der Religion,* Part 1, "Einleitung. Der Begriff der Religion," Walter Jaeschke, ed. (Hamburg: Felix Meiner, 1983), 78.

41.   See the earlier discussion of changes in later versions of the system, beginning on page 38.

42.   G. W. F. Hegel, *Vorlesungen über die Ästhetik* (*Lectures on Aesthetics*), in *Werke,* E. Moldenhauer and K. M. Michel, eds. (Frankfurt am Main: Suhrkamp Verlag, 1969-1971), vols. 13, 14, 15; vol. 13, 114. Vols. 13-15 are hereafter cited in text as AES1, AES2, and AES3, respectively.

43.   On Hegel's thesis about the "death of art," see my *Hegel's Phenomenology, Part II* (Athens: Ohio University Press, 1973), 157.

44.   G. W. F. Hegel, *Vorlesungen: Ausgewählte Nachschriften und Manuskripte,* vol. 3, *Vorlesungen über die Philosophie der Religion,* Part 1, "Ein-

leitung. Der Begriff der Religion," Walter Jaeschke, ed. (Hamburg: Felix Meiner, 1983), 3.

45. G. Nicolin, ed., *Hegel in Berichten seiner Zeitgenossen* (Hamburg: Felix Meiner, 1970), 445.

46. Aristotle, *Nicomachean Ethics* book 10, 7, 1178b.

47. G. W. F. Hegel, *Wissenschaft der Logik (Science of Logic)*, in *Werke,* E. Moldenhauer and K. M. Michel, eds. (Frankfurt am Main: Suhrkamp Verlag, 1969-1971), vol. 4, 261.

Chapter Seven

1. Benedetto Croce, *What Is Living and What Is Dead of the Philosophy of Hegel,* Douglas Ainslie, trans. (London: Macmillan, 1915). Hereafter cited in text.

2. According to the Online Computer Library Center database, 103 books were published on Hegel from 1950-1960, 230 from 1960-1970, 367 from 1970-1980, and 450 from 1980-1990.

3. An example of this reaction is to be found in Richard Norman, *Hegel's Phenomenology: A Philosophical Introduction* (New York: St. Martin's, 1976), which is one volume in the series "Philosophy Now," which is described by the publisher as "books . . . united by nothing except discontent with the narrowness and specialism of analytic philosophy. Convinced that the analytical movement has spent its momentum, its latest phase no doubt its last, the [Philosophy Now] series seeks in one way or another to push philosophy out of its ivory tower."

4. Richard Bernstein, "Why Hegel Now," *Review of Metaphysics,* vol. 31 (September 1977), 44. Hereafter cited in text.

5. See Karl Barth, *Protestant Thought,* Brian Cozens, trans. (New York: Simon & Schuster, 1969).

6. Hans Küng, *The Incarnation of God: An Introduction to Hegel's Theological Thought as a Prolegomena to a Future Christology,* J. R. Stephenson, trans. (New York: Crossword, 1987).

7. Robert Solomon, *In the Spirit of Hegel* (New York: Oxford University Press, 1983), chap. 10.

8. Examples of parallels are given in Kainz 1976, 134, 140, 146, 147-48, 150, 151, 157, 158; and my *Hegel's Phenomenology, Part II: The Evolution of Ethical and Religious Consciousness to the Absolute Standpoint,* 22, 69, 110, 170.

9. Cf., for example, Werner Becker, *Hegel's Phänomenologie des Geistes: Eine Interpretation* (Stuttgart, 1971), 140. Becker, a realist, claims that dialectic in the last analysis is an antiprogressive (conservative) methodology.

10. See, e.g., *Observations on the Feeling of the Beautiful and Sublime.* Goldthwart, trans. (Berkeley: University of California Press, 1960), 110.

11. G. W. F. Hegel, *Vorlesungen über die Philosophie des Geistes,* Franz Hespe and Burkhard Tuschling, eds. (Hamburg: Felix Meiner, 1994), 27.

Selected Bibliography

PRIMARY SOURCES

Hegel, G. W. F., *Werke in zwanzig Bänden,* E. Moldenhauer and K. M. Michel, eds. Frankfurt am Main: Suhrkamp Verlag, 1969-1971.

————, *Werke,* vol. 2: *Über die wissenshaftlichen Behandlungsarten des Naturrechts* . . . (*On the Treatment of Natural Law* . . .).

————, *Werke,* vol. 2: *Differenz des Fichteschen und Schellingschen Systems der Philosphie* (*The Difference between Schelling's and Fichte's System of Philosophy*).

————, *Werke,* vol. 2: *Glauben und Wissen* . . . (*Faith and Knowledge* . . .).

————, *Werke,* vols. 5-6: *Wissenschaft der Logik* (*Science of Logic*).

————, *Werke,* vol. 7: *Grundlinien der Philosophie des Rechts* (*Outline of the Philosophy of Right*).

————, *Werke,* vols. 8-10: *Enzyklopädie der philosophischen Wissenschaften* (*Encyclopedia of Philosophical Sciences*).

————, *Werke,* vol. 12: *Vorlesungen über die Philosophie der Geschichte* (*Lectures on the Philosophy of History*).

————, *Werke,* vols. 13-15: *Vorlesungen über die Ästhetik* (*Lectures on Aesthetics*).

————, *Werke,* vols. 16-17: *Vorlesungen über die Philosophie der Religion* (*Lectures on the Philosophy of Religion*).

————, *Werke,* vols. 18-20: *Vorlesungen über die Geschichte der Philosophie* (*Lectures on the History of Philosophy*).

————, *Phänomenologie des Geistes* (*Phenomenology of Spirit*), Hans-Friedrich Wessels and Heinrich Clairmont, eds. Hamburg: Felix Meiner Verlag, 1988.

————, *Enzyklopädie der philosophischen Wissenschaften* (*Encyclopedia of Philosophical Sciences*) 1st (Heidelberg) edition, Hermann Glockner, ed. Stuttgart: Friedrich Frommann Verlag, 1968.

————, *Hegel's Phenomenology of Spirit: Selections Translated and Annotated by Howard P. Kainz.* University Park: Pennsylvania State University Press, 1994.

————, *Vorlesungen: Ausgewählte Nachschriften und Manuskripte* (*Lectures: Selected Transcripts and Manuscripts*), vol. 5, *Vorlesungen über die Philosophie der Religion* (*Lectures on the Philosophy of Religion*), Part 3, "Die vollendete Religion" ("The Consummate Religion"), Walter Jaeschke, ed. Hamburg: Felix Meiner, 1984.

————, *Vorlesungen: Ausgewählte Nachschriften und Manuskripte* (*Lectures: Selected Transcripts and Manuscripts*), vol. 3, *Vorlesungen über die Philosophie der Religion* (*Lectures on the Philosophy of Religion*) Part 1, "Einleitung. Der Begriff der Religion" ("Introduction. The Concept of Religion"), Walter Jaeschke, ed. Hamburg: Felix Meiner, 1983.

Hegel, G. W. F., *Lectures on the History of Philosophy: The Lectures of 1825-1826,*
    vol. 3, *Medieval and Modern Philosophy,* Robert F. Brown, ed.; R. F. Brown
    and J. M. Stewart with the assistance of H. S. Harris, trans. Berkeley and
    Los Angeles: University of California Press, 1990.
————, *Vorlesungen über die Philosophie des Geistes,* Franz Hespe and Burkhard
    Tuschling, eds. Hamburg: Felix Meiner, 1994.
————, *The Berlin Phenomenology,* M. J. Petry, ed. and trans. Dordrecht: Rei-
    del, 1981.
————, *Hegel's Philosophy of Nature,* vol. 1. M. J. Petry, ed. and trans. New
    York: Humanities, 1970.
————, *Hegel's Philosophy of Subjective Spirit,* M. J. Petry, ed. and trans. Dor-
    drecht: Reidel, 1978.

SECONDARY SOURCES
Althaus, Horst, *Hegel und die heroischen Jahre der Philosophie: Eine Biographie.*
    Freiburg: Carl Hanser Verlag, 1992.
Apostolopoulou, Georgia, "Probleme der neugriechischen Hegel-Überset-
    zung," *Übersetzen, Verstehen, Brücken Bauen,* Teil 1. Berlin: Erich Schmidt
    Verlag, 1993.
Armour, Leslie, *Logic and Reality: An Investigation into the Idea of a Dialectical Sys-
    tem.* Assen: Van Gorcum, 1972.
Bernstein, Richard, "Why Hegel Now," *Review of Metaphysics,* vol. 31, 1, Sep-
    tember 1977.
Bonsiepen, Wolfgang, "Phänomenologie des Geistes," in Otto Pöggeler, *Hegel.*
    Freiburg-München: Karl Alber Verlag, 1977.
Croce, Benedetto, *What Is Living and What Is Dead of the Philosophy of Hegel,*
    Douglas Ainslie, trans. London: Macmillan, 1915.
Harris, H. S., *Hegel's Development: Towards the Sunlight, 1770-1801.* Oxford:
    Clarendon, 1972.
————, "The Hegel Renaissance in the Anglo-Saxon World Since 1945," *The
    Owl of Minverva,* vol. 15, 1, Fall 1983.
Hösle, Vittorio, *Hegels System: Der Idealismus der Subjektivität und das Problem der
    Intersubjektivität.* Hamburg: Felix Meiner Verlag, 1988.
Kainz, Howard, *Paradox, Dialectic and System: A Contemporary Reconstruction of the
    Hegelian Problematic.* University Park: Pennsylvania State University
    Press, 1988.
————, *Hegel's Phenomenology, Part II: The Evolution of Ethical and Religious Con-
    sciousness to the Absolute Standpoint.* Athens: Ohio University Press, 1973.
————, *Hegel's* Phenomenology, *Part I: Analysis and Commentary.* Tuscaloosa:
    University of Alabama Press, 1976.
McRae, Robert Grant, *Philosophy and the Absolute.* The Hague: Nijhoff, 1985.
Melhuish, George, *The Paradoxical Nature of Reality.* Bristol: St. Vincent's,
    1973.

Pöggeler, Otto, *Hegels Idee einer Phänomenologie des Geistes.* Freiburg/München: Karl Abler Verlag, 1973.

Souche-Dagues, Denise, *Le circle hégélien.* Paris: Presses Universitaires de France, 1986.

Toms, Eric, *Being, Negation and Logic.* Oxford: Basil Blackwell, 1962.

Wandschneider, Dieter, *Raum, Zeit, Relativität: Grundbestimmungen der Physik in der Perspecktive der Hegelschen Naturphilosophie.* Frankfurt am Main: Vittorio Klostermann, 1982.

Wiedmann, Franz, *Hegel: An Illustrated Biography,* J. Neugroschel, trans. New York: Pegasus, 1968.

Index

The Author

Howard Kainz has been a professor at Marquette University, Milwaukee, since 1967. He was a recipient of an NEH fellowship for 1977–1978 and Fulbright fellowships in Germany for 1980–1981 and 1987–1988. His major publications include *Hegel's Phenomenology, Part I: Analysis and Commentary* (1976), *Ethica Dialectica: A Study of Ethical Oppositions* (1979), *Hegel's Phenomenology, Part II: The Evolution of Ethical and Religious Consciousness to the Absolute Standpoint* (1973), *Philosophical Perspectives on Peace* (1987), *Ethics in Context: Toward the Definition and Differentiation of the Morally Good* (1988), *Paradox, Dialectic and System: A Reconstruction of the Hegelian Problematic* (1988), *Democracy and the "Kingdom of God"* (1993), and *Hegel's Phenomonology of Spirit: Selections Translated and Annotated by Howard P. Kainz* (1994). His *Paradox, Dialectic and System* received the *Choice* Distinguished Scholarly Book award for 1988. He plays the piano, bikes, plays racquetball, and surfs the Internet, where he is a frequent participant in the Hegel discussion group located at Hegel-l@bucknell.edu.

The Editor

David O'Connell is professor of French at Georgia State University. He received his Ph.D. in 1966 from Princeton University, where he was a National Woodrow Wilson Fellow, the Bergen Fellow in Romance Languages, and a National Woodrow Wilson Dissertation Fellow. He is the author of *The Teachings of Saint Louis: A Critical Text* (1972), *Les Propos de Saint Louis* (1974), *Louis-Ferdinand Céline* (1976), *The Instructions of Saint Louis: A Critical Text* (1979), and *Michel de Saint Pierre: A Catholic Novelist at the Crossroads* (1990). He has edited more than sixty books in the Twayne World Authors Series.